THE STATE ACTING ACADEMY OF EAST BERLIN–
A HISTORY OF ACTOR TRAINING FROM
MAX REINHART'S *SCHAUSPIELSCHULE* TO *THE
HOCHSCHULE FÜR SCHAUSPIELKUNST "ERNST BUSCH"*

THE STATE ACTING ACADEMY OF EAST BERLIN—
A HISTORY OF ACTOR TRAINING FROM MAX REINHART'S *SCHAUSPIELSCHULE* TO *THE HOCHSCHULE FÜR SCHAUSPIELKUNST "ERNST BUSCH"*

Steve Earnest

Studies in Theatre Arts
Volume 7

The Edwin Mellen Press
Lewiston•Queenston•Lampeter

Library of Congress Cataloging-in-Publication Data

Earnest, Steve.
  The state acting academy of East Berlin : a history of actor
training from Max Reinhardt's Schauspielschule to the Hochschule für
Schauspielkunst "Ernst Busch" / Steve Earnest.
      p.   cm. -- (Studies in theatre arts ; v. 7)
  Includes bibliographical references and index.
  ISBN 0-7734-7916-3
  1. Hochschule für Schauspielkunst "Ernst Busch"--History.
 2. Acting--Study and teaching--Germany--Berlin.   I. Title.
 II. Series.
PN2078.G42B475   1999
792'.028' 071043155--dc21   99-33840
                                                                    CIP

This is volume 7 in the continuing series
Studies in Theatre Arts
Volume 7 ISBN 0-7734-7916-3
STA Series ISBN 0-7734-9721-8

A CIP catalog record for this book is available from the British Library.

Copyright © 1999 Steve Earnest

All rights reserved. For information contact

          The Edwin Mellen Press   The Edwin Mellen Press
                Box 450   Box 67
          Lewiston, New York   Queenston, Ontario
            USA 14092-0450   CANADA L0S 1L0

                The Edwin Mellen Press, Ltd.
                Lampeter, Ceredigion, Wales
                UNITED KINGDOM SA48 8LT

            Printed in the United States of America

Contents

PREFACE i
ACKNOWLEDGEMENTS v
INTRODUCTION 1
    Justification for the Study 1
    Methods of Research 3
    The German Acting Profession 6

1. THE DEVELOPMENT OF THEATRE, THE ACTOR,
    AND ACTOR TRAINING 15
    Theatre in the Germanic Region 15
    Gottsched and Neuber - Early Reforms 17
    Ekhof and the Beginnings of Acting Theory 18
    The Hamburg Dramaturgy - Lessings' Theoretical Statement 20
    Schroeder, Iffland and Devrient Romantic Acting Styles 22
    Goethe and the Weimar School 25
    Eduard Devrient 28
    Schreyvogel and Saxe-Meiningen:the Ensemble Approach 29
    Development of Acting Styles in the Twentieth Century 33
    Antirealistic Acting 35

2. MAX REINHARDT AND THE SCHAUSPIELSCHULE
    DES DEUTSCHEN THEATERS 41

    Max Reinhardt 41

    Reinhardt's Theatrical Vision 46

    Reinhardt's Work With Actors 47

    Founding of the Schauspielschule 50

    The Schauspielschule 1910 - 1935 53

    The Schauspielschule in the Third Reich 56

3.   DEVELOPMENT OF EAST GERMAN AESTHETICS 61

    German Theatre After the War 61

    The German Democratic Republic 62

    Socialist Realism in the U.S.S.R. 65

    The Development of East German Theatre Aesthetics 68

    Stanislavski - The Model for Performance 71

    Bertolt Brecht - The "Other" Approach 75

4.   STAATLICHE SCHAUSPIELSCHULE BERLIN 79

    State Academies Established 79

    Staatliche Schauspielschule Berlin 81

    Program of Study at the State Acting Academy 85

    Leadership of the State Acting Academy (1962 - 1989) 87

    Work With Brecht and Stanislavski 89

    Hans-Peter Minetti 92

5. THE HOCHSCHULE FÜR SCHAUSPIELKUNST "ERNST BUSCH" 97

   Part I. Hochschule Status and the Eighties 97

      Ernst Busch 97

      German Reunification 100

   Part II. Theatre Training in 1992-93 105

      Facilities for Instruction 106

         Schöneweide Campus 106

         studiotheater BAT 109

         Theater Am Park 110

      Curriculum 111

         Acting 111

         Speech Training 119

         Movement 122

         Theater Science 125

         Directing 126

         Choreography 128

6. ACTORS PRESENT AND PAST - STUDENT PERSPECTIVES OF THE HOCHSCHULE FÜR SCHAUSPIELKUNST "ERNST BUSCH" 131

   Student Body 131

   Student Perception of the Acting Program 136

   Employment Prospects 138

   Former Students - Reactions to the Program 140

	Dieter Mann	140
	Christine Schorn	142
	Frank Lienert	143
	Daniel Morgenroth	145
7.	CONCLUSION	149
	Evaluation of the HfSK	149
	Suggestions for Further Study	159

APPENDICES 163

BIBLIOGRAPHY 167

INDEX 175

PREFACE

The theatre of Germany shares with Russia and America an 18th-century birthdate as an organized and nationally distinctive enterprise. And like Russia, but unlike America, one of the earliest indicators of the emergence of such an enterprise was the establishment of a school for actors, the Schönemann Academy, founded by the actor Konrad Ekhof in 1753.

Since that time, German actors, theorists, and directors have joined with their European and American counterparts in the ongoing discussions about the actor's craft and the means of developing it. In the late eighteenth century, Lessing was not impressed with what he saw on the stage of the Hamburg National Theatre. "We have actors but no art of acting," he wrote in the Hamburg Dramaturgy. Some thirty years later, Goethe sought to improve the quality of acting at the Duke of Weimar's theatre through his "Rules for Actors," which included the admonition, "First, the player must reflect that he must not only imitate Nature, but must also present her ideally." Styles and tastes changed over the next century and by 1929 Max Reinhardt felt compelled to write, "The modern social code has crippled the actor, whose business it is to body forth feeling. . . . How can the actor, rooted deep in the bourgeois existence of every-day, suddenly in the evening leap into the life of the mad king, whose unrestrained passion sweeps like a storm across the moors?" How indeed? For Piscator and Brecht, the answer was to be found in Epic Theatre. "Whoever has told you that you can shut yourself off behind an imaginary 'fourth wall' has misinformed you," was Piscator's warning to the actor. "You have a mission. Your mission is to entertain me and while you are entertaining me you also have to be my teacher."

From Goethe's actor who should reflect Nature "ideally" to Piscator's actor-as-teacher, the German theatre has bodied forth, and at times prompted, our changing ideas in the western world about the proper role of the actor on the stage. In his study of one of the leading theatre schools of twentieth century Germany, the *Hochschule für Schauspielkunst "Ernst Busch,"* Stephen Earnest draws upon a wealth of documentary evidence and personal visits to the Berlin (formerly East Berlin) school to lay before us not only the historical development of the school through Germany's tumultuous twentieth century, but also a detailed account of the present inner workings of this academy. Obviously, the story of any institution's endurance through World War I, Hitler's Third Reich, and Soviet hegemony is a story of survival through accommodation and tenacity. Now, at the end of the century, the school seeks to address the changing aesthetic demands of the postmodern theatre, while at the same time making the necessary adjustments from life under dictatorial communism to life within the hurly-burly of global capitalism.

A study such as this is not just an examination of a training program for would-be theatre professionals, as one might expect from an examination of one of the many MFA programs in the United States. In Germany, as in other European countries, serious theatre training takes place in vocational schools for the performing arts—in Germany, the theatre *Hochschule*. The *Hochschule für Schauspielkunst "Ernst Busch"* is one of but fourteen such schools in Germany. At *Ernst Busch*, the admission ratio into the acting program is approximately one out of each fifteen auditioners—and the auditioners are preselected from a much larger number of applicants. First year students at such institutions are usually in their mid-twenties with several years of performing experience in school and amateur theatre groups.

The school retains close connections with the *Deutsches Theater*, for over a century one of Germany's leading theatres. The *Deutsches* was founded in 1883 for the expressed purpose of providing Berlin with an ensemble company comparable to the *Meininger* Company. In 1894, Otto Brahm assumed directorship of the theatre and began promoting the idea of theatrical naturalism, including naturalistic acting. Ten years later a former member of Brahm's company, Max Reinhardt, succeeded Brahm as artistic director. Within a year, Reinhardt opened a training academy affiliated with the theatre, and it is from this academy that the *Hochschule für Schauspielkunst "Ernst Busch"* traces its lineage.

Appropriately, Professor Earnest begins his interesting and informative study with an examination Reinhardt's artistic vision and the actor's place in that vision. After surviving World War II and coming under the domination of Soviet Russia, the theatres and training programs of East Germany entered an interesting and rather dichotomous period in which an effort was made to accommodate the aesthetics of socialist realism (promoted as Stanislavsky-based) with the epic theatre philosophy of the most celebrated German director and theorist since Reinhardt, Bertolt Brecht. At this point Professor Earnest introduces us to Rudolf Penka, a Czech-born, German educated actor and teacher who, in 1961, was appointed Director of the State Acting Academy (as the school was then known). For the next fourteen years Penka developed an approach to actor training that adroitly synthesized the theories of Stanislavsky and Brecht. He was replaced as Director in 1975, but continued to teach at the school until his death in 1990.

In 1981 the State Acting Academy of East Berlin was relocated into new quarters and renamed the *Hochschule für Schauspielkunst "Ernst Busch."* Ernst Busch was one of Brecht's favorite actors and a prominent member of the Communist Party. This tilt towards Brecht and political correctness characterized the school in the 1980s until the wall literally came tumbling down in 1989. In 1992, Professor Earnest made his first of two visits to the *Hochschule* and began his investigation into the school, its history, and its place and influence in the German theatre of today.

Many of the actors currently employed at three of Berlin's leading theatres—the *Deutsches Theater*, the *Berliner Ensemble*, and the *Maxim Gorki Theater*—received their training at the *Hochschule für Schauspielkunst "Ernst Busch."* During his second visit to Berlin, Professor Earnest learned that of the 163 actors employed at these three theatres for the 1992-1993 season, 77 (47%) had been trained at the *Hochschule "Ernst Busch."* This, as well as its longevity, speaks to the importance of the Hochschule in the history of twentieth-century German theatre. It is an idea somewhat foreign to American theatre: that there should be a conscious interrelatedness between the training of theatre artists and the professed theatre aesthetic of a theatre, a group of theatres, or even a nation. Yet, that is the journey, haphazard at times, through the twentieth century of this particular academy. And in charting this journey, Stephen Earnest offers us not only the story of a particular training institution, but insights as well from an uncommon perspective on twentieth-century German theatre.

James M. Symons
Professor and Chair of Theatre and Dance
University of Colorado, Boulder

ACKNOWLEDGEMENTS

    I would like to thank the following people for their guidance and support with this project: the faculty, staff and students of the *Hochschule für Schauspielkunst "Ernst Busch,"* especially Professor Kurt Veth, Ulrich Engelmann, Herbert Minnich, Wolfgang Rodler, Veronica Drogi, Klaus and Gertrud Klawitter, Klaus Völker, Ursula Schultze, and Peter Kleinert. I would like to thank the following students for their personal views regarding the program at the *Hochschule*: Jeff Burrell, Thomas Mathys, Matthais Bundschue and Ron Speiss. Thanks also to *frau* Angelika Gützkow and the following actors of the *Deutsches Theater*: Dieter Mann, Christine Schorn, Frank Lienert and Daniel Morgenroth for allowing me to interview them. Support for this project was provided by Dean Rodney Taylor of the University of Colorado and Dean Michel Simoneaux of Palm Beach Atlantic College. I would like to thank Yvonne Shafer for her help in arranging contact with the HfSK and also recognize the late Hugo Schmidt for his help with translating several of my early documents. Additional help with translation was provided by Judy Schaffer of Boulder, Colorado, and John Dawes of Palm Beach Atlantic College.
  Special thanks to Dr. Thomas Engel of the German Center of the International Theatre Institute for providing me with several important facts about the German theatre system.
  Above all, I credit the success of this project to my dissertation advisor and good friend, Dr. James Symons of the University of Colorado.

INTRODUCTION

In November of 1989 the demolition of the Berlin Wall began, signifying the end of the German Democratic Republic and setting in motion a massive post-communist effort to reunify the two Germanys. The new Germany would consist of the former Federal Republic of Germany plus the six (6) *Neue Bundeslander*, or states, which comprised the former German Democratic Republic. With this reunification came the merger of governmental entities, businesses, currencies, educational systems, and state supported theatre systems.

During the past two hundred years, Germany has developed an enormous state supported theatre system. As of 1993 there were some two hundred and seven state supported theatre companies in a country approximately the size of Oregon. Within this system as many as five thousand actors, singers and dancers are employed on a yearly basis. In order to provide the system with a constant supply of *Nachwuchs*, or young recruits, the country of Germany has organized a network of official theatre training programs to guarantee high quality artists needed to fill these positions.

Justification for this Study

For most theatre professionals and academics in America, knowledge of German theatre training programs is limited. However, for that same group of people, interest in and/or knowledge of German theatre is in most cases fairly high. Most are familiar with the work of the Duke of Saxe-Meiningen, Max Reinhardt,

Bertolt Brecht, and perhaps Heiner Müller. We are knowledgeable about the careers of a few famous German actors and actresses, such as Marlene Dietrich, Helene Weigel, and Peter Lorre. But the vast majority of German stage personnel, and the system for training them, is largely unknown. Should this remain so? Can it not be said that one of the best ways to glean knowledge about the inner workings of a particular country's theatre system is to observe the way in which it educates and trains future theatre artists? Certainly history would indicate that it is. Although there are few examples of schools that have existed apart from resident companies, there are many examples of training institutions which have been related to producing organizations. We have learned a great deal about the approach to theatre in Russia by looking at the work in the studio programs of the Moscow Art Theatre. Similar cases can be made for the *Comédie Française*, the Group Theatre, and Grotowski's Polish Laboratory Theatre, which, strictly speaking, were or became theatre companies with schools attached. By looking at a German institution such as the *Hochschule für Schauspielkunst "Ernst Busch" (HfSK)*, which will later be shown to warrant the title of a model German theater training institution, we as theater scholars can extend our knowledge of German Theatre and, as teachers of acting and other performance disciplines, we can gain insight into and learn from this proven system.

    Because the *HfSK* is located in the former German Democratic Republic, very little is known of it outside of Germany. Therefore, most information must be gathered directly from the source, making this the first English Language study to have done so. A 1978 dissertation by Bruce Matley of Wayne State University concerned actor training at two schools in West Germany, but it did not include East Germany or any of the areas in and around Berlin, which is considered the theatrical capital of Germany.

    The *HfSK*, known from 1951 to 1981 as the *Staatliche Schauspielschule Berlin*, can be justifiably designated as a model German theatre training institution for several reasons: first, it is the direct descendant of the *Schauspielschule* (or acting school) of the *Deutsches Theater*. Established in 1905 by Max Reinhardt, the *Schauspielschule* was one of the first organized attempts in Germany during the modern era to provide training for actors and other theatre personnel. Secondly, the *HfSK* is located in Berlin, the theatrical capital of Germany, and is tightly intertwined with the Berlin theatre system. For over thirty years there has been a continuous record of employment for graduates of the *HfSK*, both during and after completion of their studies, with major theatres in Berlin, such as the *Deutsches Theater*, the *Maxim Gorki Theater*, the *Berliner Ensemble*, and the *Komische Oper*. In fact, of the 163 actors employed during the 1992-93 season by the first three theatres mentioned above, 77 were trained at the *HfSK*. There has also been an on-going system of exchange in the area of artistic personnel between the *HfSK* and those same major theatres. It is not uncommon to find Berlin's major directors and acting coaches teaching master classes at the *HfSK* or directing advanced students in studio projects. In contrast to their non-academic attitude and focus, the faculty at the *HfSK* has maintained a record of publication devoted to the practical discussion of performance theory, primarily the art of acting. Finally, the *HfSK* has developed a strong acting program, based initially on the work of Max Reinhardt, and later expanded to encompass the theories of Konstantin Stanislavski, Bertolt Brecht, and others. It has been and continues to be exemplary in its constant analysis of the practice and evolution of the art of theatre.

Methods of Research

Information that documents actor training in the former eastern sector of Germany is very scarce. Although there is a fair amount of material concerning actor training and acting theory published in German, previously it has not been available to American scholars and teachers of acting who do not speak German. Additionally, very little of the material published in Germany is empirical, i.e. based on actual practice, from the objective standpoint of an observer. Because of the practical needs of this study, the author made two trips to what was formerly the city of East Berlin, to conduct on-site research at the *HfSK*. During the first visit, for ten days in May of 1992, I met the faculty, staff, and many students from the *HfSK*, attended several classes and rehearsal periods at the institution, conducted interviews with certain key faculty members, and collected materials and books not available in the United States.

During the second visit, for one month in May of 1993, I conducted more extensive interviews with faculty and students, arranged and conducted interviews with former students of the *HfSK* now working professionally, and engaged in longer periods of observation. I gathered information from the students regarding the approaches to theatre training at the *HfSK*, how the program had changed (if any) during reunification, how the program influenced their careers, and strengths and weaknesses of the program. Interviews with the professors revealed information regarding approaches and methodologies in their individual disciplines.

During my visits to Germany and through correspondence with several libraries in the United States, previously published material was gathered which dealt with the history and philosophy of theatre training in Germany and at the *HfSK*. To supplement this, I located other published material which discussed various aspects of theatre training in the former GDR, the training program at the *Staatliche Schauspielschule Berlin*, and interviews with particular actors and/or professors. Aside from two articles which were "jobbed out," I have translated all of this material myself.

The structure of the monograph is as follows. Chapter one will serve as the introduction, and will include items such as the need, justification, methodology, and parameters of the study. Additionally, chapter one will discuss the German theatre system, how it works, and how performers enter the system. Chapter two will provide a historical overview of theatre training (specifically actor training) in Germany. It will begin with Johann Gottsched and Caroline Neuber and the "Leipzig

School of Acting" and will continue in a chronological manner through the early 20th Century. Chapter three will discuss the *Schauspielschule des Deutschen Theaters* - the first of the major influences on the *HfSK*. Initially the early work of Max Reinhardt will be analyzed, including his decision to found an acting school. The school's training approach, curriculum, and teachers will be discussed, with the years 1905 - 1944 included. The chapter will end with the halt of organized theatrical activity during World War II. Chapter four will include material relating to East German aesthetics, because methodology and theoretical concerns were so important to the East German system. The point of departure will be socialist realism in both Russia and the German Democratic Republic. The emphasis will then shift to Stanislavski and Brecht and the influence they have commanded over East German performance aesthetics. Chapter five will discuss the *Staatliche Schauspielschule Berlin*, which was created from the tradition of the *Schauspielschule des Deutschen Theaters*. The establishment of theatre training institutes in the GDR will be covered, followed by an analysis of the philosophy and curriculum of the *Staatliche Schauspielschule*. Chapter six will look at the school as it was in 1993 - the *HfSK*. With chapter six the study moves inside the school and discusses the facilities, curriculum, philosophy of instruction, faculty, and students. This chapter will include a discussion concerning the transition from an institution of the German Democratic Republic to an institution in a unified Germany. The faculty and curriculum will be analyzed with emphasis on the changes that occurred between 1989 and 1993. Chapter seven will include material relating to the impact of the "Ernst Busch" school: the actors produced by the school. Information from and about 1993 students will be presented, based on interviews and published writings. Emphasis will be on the perception of students, what they expected and what they received, and/or expectations for the future. Chapter eight will serve as the conclusion.

The German Acting Profession

Before discussing the history of German actor training, and the program at the *HfSK* it will be beneficial to include a brief section about Germany's system for training actors and other artists. First, it should be clarified that the information contained in this section relates to Germany in 1993 - as opposed to the early twentieth century or the GDR (1949-1989). Although there were changes taking place even as this study was being written (1994), it is accurate to say that the system for training actors in Germany resembled that which had been in existence in West Germany since 1949. As of 1994, most of the East German schools still existed in one form or another, but had been usurped by the educational system of the Federal Republic of Germany.

If one has the dream and aspiration to become a professional actor in Germany, it is not a realistic option, as it is in the United States, to simply enroll at a university, become a performing arts major, and hope to have a career in professional theatre. While most German universities have divisions of theatre, and many have practicing drama clubs, the approach taken by German universities is primarily academic, and one would not receive training in the performance skills necessary to tackle the demanding German repertory system. Most successful German actors and actresses have completed a program at a theatre *Hochschule*, a vocational school for the performing arts. Though it is possible in to obtain a contract with a major theatre company without a diploma from a *Hochschule* as of 1994 it had become increasingly rare, and those who had not received training from a theatre *Hochschule* generally did not have the same mobility and longevity in their careers as those with vocational training. This statement is based on information gathered from interviews conducted with staff members and professional actors and actresses at both the *Deutsches Theater*, the *Berliner Ensemble* and with students and faculty members of the *HfSK*.

As of 1994 there were fourteen major institutions in Germany that specialized in training actors and performing personnel. Several included divisions for training in film and television acting, but most emphasized careers on the stage. A listing of all the German schools appears at the end of this chapter. All fourteen are official, state supported theatre institutions, designed to give vocational instruction in the performing arts. Vocational schools (and other educational institutions, such as universities) are not accredited in Germany in the same manner that they are in the United States. Accreditation of lower level university degrees (i.e. *Diplom* and *Magister*) is the responsibility of the individual states of Germany: Baden-Wurtemburg, Bavaria, Bremen, Hamburg, Hesse, Lower Saxony, North Rhine-Westphalia, Rhineland-Palatinate, Saarland, Schleswig, West Berlin, and all the recently reintegrated states of what was East Germany. According to Caspar von Rex, superintendent of the *HfSK*, each institute is responsible for its own internal analysis and governance. However, the institutes are subject to close scrutiny by one of several governing boards. The most important of these is the Council of Sciences, or *Wissenschaftsrat*. The Council makes recommendations for the structural and curricular development of the universities and technical schools, and on the organization and promotion of science and research. The Council also conducts periodic audits/observations of the institutes and provides the institute with written notification of its recommendations. These are not taken lightly by the institutions; continued funding is contingent on satisfactory evaluation by the Council of Sciences. The Council also decides, as it did in the case of the *Institut für Musik und Theater des Landes Mecklenburg-Vorpommern*, if and when schools of drama and music need to be eliminated or combined with other similar schools due to financial constraints. As of 1994 the only theatre school that had been closed or merged was the *Staatliche Schauspielschule Rostock*.

On average, the student to faculty ratio at German theatre training institutions is 4:1, an extraordinarily low figure when compared to that faced by theatre educators in the United States, who are occasionally faced with ratios approaching 20:1.[1] In order to be considered for acceptance into a theater *Hochschule*, students must hold an *Abitur*, a German secondary school certificate, or in the case of foreign students a recognized foreign equivalent (for applicants from the United States a high school diploma is sufficient). Foreign students must speak fluent German in order to be considered for acceptance, since all instruction is in German. Students pay no tuition at the state schools. Like all post-secondary educational institutions in Germany, the theatre schools are state-run, non-profit institutions. In addition, students who are accepted are entitled to a *BaFog* (or stipend) to cover their living expenses. As of 1994 the process for awarding stipends was undergoing changes, but averaged around 800dm per student monthly for German nationals. Non-German students are not entitled to a stipend, and must make financial arrangements through their home country or sponsor.

In addition to the academic requirements, students must pass an audition before being accepted into a theatre *Hochschule*. Generally, this consists of the auditionee performing two contrasting monologues, usually singing a song, and in some cases, reciting prose. Because of the incredibly large number of applicants, these auditions are held on a weekly basis throughout the academic year. Final auditions, or callbacks, are held in March of each year. Those accepted are notified in May.[2]

It is extremely difficult to gain admission into any one of the state institutes. For instance, at the *HfSK* well over 1000 applications are received each year. Out of these, around half are allowed to audition. Only thirty students are accepted into the acting program each year. Competition is even stiffer for other

---

[1] Information taken from the Directory of Theatre Training Programs II, Jill Charles, Ed. Published by Theatre Dictionaries, 1989. Information surveyed showed that while most university theatre departments in the United States maintain a student/faculty ratio of about 10:1, several major institutions have a ratio approaching 20:1. The most notable of these is the University of Texas at Austin, with a 19:1 ratio.
[2] This is the procedure at the *Hochschule für Schauspielkunst "Ernst Busch."*

programs within the *HfSK*, as far fewer students are accepted into directing and choreography programs.[3]

After completing all degree requirements, theatre students are awarded a *Diplom*, basically the equivalent of a Bachelor of Fine Arts degree (minus the liberal arts component) from an American institution. However, given the nature of the training that takes place and the level of maturity of the students, it can be argued that the degree received by graduates of a theatre *Hochschule* has the same worth as a M.F.A. degree from an American University theatre department. Certainly, when one compares the intense training received by students of a German theatre *Hochschule* to an American M.F.A. program, the two are strikingly similar.[4]

The next logical task is attempting to secure a position with a theatre company or with a television or film production company. This study focuses primarily on training for the stage, but apparently employment in film and television is much like that in the United States: actors are hired on a project by project basis. The primary difference lies in the fact that there are no private agents or management organizations in Germany. The association responsible for placement of actors and other artistic personnel is the *Genossenschaft Deutscher Buhnenangehorigen (GDBA)*, in many ways the German equivalent of Actor's Equity Association. Founded in 1871 in Weimar, the *GDBA* is the main union of actors and technicians working within theatre companies. The *GDBA* provides insurance, legal protection for actors, and a publishing company, the *Bühnenschriften-Vertriebsgesellschaft m.b.H* in Hamburg. The *GDBA* maintains listings of actors, and attempts to arrange for placement; but in actuality much of that is done through contacts, open castings, and senior-level *hochschule* projects that are attended by casting directors. Many

---

[3]Herbert Minnich, Pro-Rektor, interview conducted in Berlin, Germany, May 1993.
[4]This is a personal observation. Three reasons for this opinion: students at the German schools are usually older and more mature than American undergraduate students; the nature of the program is much more practical than B.F.A. programs, which have a core requirement of 35-50 classes; for actors, a *Diplom* carries the same weight as a terminal degree. Many German possess the *Diplom* as their sole teaching credential.

students are hired and begin working before they actually graduate, and several obtain theatre and film contracts during their matriculation.[5]

Another agency that assists in the placement of actors is the Central Theatre Agency or *Zentrale Bühnen-Fernseh- und Filmvermittlung der Bundesanstalt für Arbeit* (*ZBF*). The *ZBF* is a governmental agency maintained by the labor exchange that assists in the placement of actors in television, movies, and large musical productions.

The basic contract for a German actor is the called the *Normalvertrag Solo* or Standard Solo Contract. A typical contract with a professional theatre company, such as the *Deutsches Theater*, lasts for an initial period of three years.[6] At the *Deutsches Theater*, this is simply a matter of philosophy -- because they attempt to function as a tight-knit ensemble, they wish to allow a group of performers to work together for a longer period of time than just a single season. This also relieves the performer from the stress of wondering whether or not he or she will be employed during the next season or not and they can devote all of their mental faculties to what they are paid to do, act. So, in order to be hired as a company member at a large repertory theatre like the *Deutsches Theater*, an actor must prove that he/she is worthy of a three-year stint. After the initial three-year contract, however, companies exercise one of three options. First, they can offer the actor another three-year contract, which is the case with the majority of performers. Second, they may elect to offer the actor a one-year contract. Sometimes this is just a matter of casting, and changes in the repertoire may dictate alternative casting needs. Frequently, in present day Germany, there are economic reasons influencing the employment of company members. More and more, state supported theatres, particularly in Berlin, are being forced to acknowledge the box office as a determinant for repertoire and casting

---

[5]Daniel Morgenroth, actor at the *Deutsches Theater*. Interview conducted in Berlin, Germany, May 1993.
[6]This is the custom, but not the rule. Information is based on interviews with several actors at the *Deutsches Theater*, all of whom were given three-year contracts initially. However, they stated that occasionally an actor may be given a one-year contract at the discretion of the *Intendant*.

decisions.[7] In some cases, actors simply do not fit within a company, are at odds with the management, or are not judged competent performers. In such cases performers contracts are not renewed. Other times, actors themselves refuse contracts for other offers or to pursue personal projects.[8]

Salaries for actors at the larger state theatres are good, especially when one considers the length of contract and working conditions. A first contract for an actor who has just graduated from a theatre *Hochschule* would normally amount to 1250 *Deutsche Marks* weekly, about 5000 *marks* monthly, which, in 1993 was equal to approximately $3,400 American dollars a month. The monthly payment scale for established actors is negotiated by the actor and the theatre, and ranges from 4,500 *marks* at medium sized theatres to 7,000 *marks* at larger theatres, such as the *Schaubühne am Lehniner Platz* or the *Deutsches Theater*. Later contacts may be considerably higher, with even moderately popular actors commanding salaries of 15,000 to 25,000 *deutsche marks* monthly.[9] Film contacts are even better - German actors working in major projects are paid in excess of 1000 marks a day.[10] Actors under contract are supplied with health and pension insurance. Both are obligatory and require the actor to pay half of the monthly premium.[11]

In addition to being a full company member, an actor can perform as a *Gast* (guest) actor, taking only a few roles within the company's repertoire. As a rule, company members maintain at least seven roles at any one time, while a *Gast* may have two or three roles. Occasionally a performer may elect to shift to *Gast* status while he or she is making a career change to directing or choreography, or begins to work at another theatre. Some performers refuse to attach themselves to a particular

---

[7] Ulrich Engelmann, Berlin, Germany, May 1993.

[8] Frank Lienert, Berlin, Germany, May 1993.

[9] Daniel Morgenroth, Berlin, Germany, May 1993. This is common knowledge among actors in Berlin, and many others were able to support the reliability of these figures.

[10] Jeff Burrell, Berlin Germany, May 1993.

[11] Much of this information was supplied by Dr. Thomas Engel, Assistant Director of the International Theatre Institute - German Center, Berlin.

company, opting instead to perform as a *Gast* at several theatres simultaneously.[12] This, however, is rare, and somewhat difficult, given the rotating nature of the German repertory system. Compensation for a *Gast* is negotiated between the actor and the theatre.

The reader should be aware that during 1994, many changes were taking place in the German theatre system. Employment, box office revenues, and state subsidies were areas that were under discussion, and likely to change. These facts do, however, illustrate the vastly different system that exists in Germany as compared with that of the United States. Once accepted into a theatre training program, a student has a good shot at "making it" as a professional actor. In fact, it can be said that the deciding factor in an aspiring actor's life is whether or not he or she is accepted into a training program. Student actors are subsidized during their education, and do not have to worry about securing part-time jobs to pay their tuition or rent. Taking on outside jobs during a student's matriculation is discouraged and can result in expulsion from a program. After graduation, there are no student loans to repay, and financial security is ensured by lengthy contracts with ample time for planning. In Germany, the theatre is an honored cultural institution, and actors and other artistic personnel are considered to be well educated, highly trained artists of the highest caliber.

---

[12]Frank Lienert, Berlin, Germany, May 1993.

Table 1.1

THEATRE TRAINING INSTITITIONS IN GERMANY (1994)

Hochschule der Künste Berlin
Fasanenstrasse 1
1000 Berlin 12

Hochschule für Schauspielkunst "Ernst Busch" Berlin
Schnellerstrasse 104
0-1190 Berlin

Westfälische Schauspielschule
Lohring 20
4630 Bochum 1

Folkwang-Hochschule für Musik, Theater, Tanz
Klemensborn 39
4300 Essen 16

Hochschule für Musik und Theater
Harvester Weg 12
2000 Hamburg 13

Hochschule für Musik und Theater
Emmichplatz 1
3000 Hannover

Theaterhochschule
"Hans Otto"
Schwägrichenstrasse 3
0-7010 Leipzig

Hochschule für Musik und Theater "Felix Mendelssohn Bartholdy" PSF 809
Grassisstrasse 1
0-7010 Leipzig

Otto-Falckenberg-Schule
Hildegardstrasse 3
8000 München 22

Hochschule für Film und Fernsehen "Konrad Wolf"
Karl-Marx-Strasse 33/34
0-1591 Potsdam

Hochschule für Musik und Theater
Studiengang Schauspiel
Augustenstrasse 116-117
0-2500 Rostock

Institute für Musik und Theater des Landes Mecklenburg-Vorpommern
Schillerplatz 2
0-2500 Rostock

Musikhochschule des Saarlandes
66 Saarbrücken 3
Bismarkstrasse 1

Staatliche Hochschule für Musik und darstellende Kunst
Urbansplatz 2
7000 Stuttgart 1

CHAPTER 1

THE DEVELOPMENT OF THEATRE, THE ACTOR, AND ACTOR TRAINING IN GERMANY

Initially, this chapter will provide an overview of the development of the Germanic region and the early theatrical forms that pervaded the loosely connected provinces. The discussion will eventually lead to the establishment of court theatres, and the forms of performance that developed within them. Finally, this chapter will explore the development of the resident company, since it was within the companies that actors would begin to develop methods for providing training for themselves and future generations of performers.

Theatre in the Germanic Region

Prior to the eighteenth century there were no meaningful attempts to establish a theatrical tradition in the area of northern Europe now classified as Germany. In fact, even into the nineteenth century, this area existed as a series of principalities, kingdoms, and individual cities, with little co-operative interrelationship. Religious division was created by the Reformation and counter-Reformation, eventually leading to war. The Thirty Years War, as it was known, lasted until the mid-seventeenth century with its effects plaguing the region for at least another 150 years. Resulting from this chaotic period was a very fragmented development of learning and, for the purposes of this study, of theatre.

This is not to say that theatrical attempts had not been made, and quite successfully, in northern Europe. Medieval drama had flourished in the Germanic region, which was then part of the Holy Roman Empire. In fact, only France had a stronger liturgical drama than did the areas that now constitute Germany, Switzerland, and Austria. Perhaps the greatest legacy of the German Medieval period is Hrosvitha. A nun from the imperial convent of Gandersheim in northern Germany, Hrosvitha wrote six plays (c. 1501 publication) inspired by the works of Terence. Her six plays, all of which survive, dramatize spiritual conflict and the triumph of Christian values. Hrosvitha is considered by most scholars to have been the first female playwright in the history of dramatic literature.

War ravaged the region throughout the sixteenth century and created conditions that remained unsettled well into the seventeenth century. For this reason, the Germanic region lagged behind the rest of Europe in its cultural development for the next two centuries. One of the best known practitioners of this period was Hans Sachs (1494 -1576), a shoemaker/poet who promoted Renaissance ideas in the region. Sachs is believed to have written at least 168 plays during his lifetime, most of them folk farces, or Shrovetide plays. Sachs also attempted tragedy, writing <u>Lucretia</u> (1527) and <u>Virginia</u> (1530). His travels as a solo performer and storyteller extended his influence throughout the region. Another positive development was the Academy Theatre at Strassburg. Headed by Johannes Sturm (1538 - 81), the academy provided instruction in Aristotelian and Horatian poetics and offered productions of Greek and Roman tragedies.[1] Activity at the academy continued well into the seventeenth century, when it was eventually usurped by the Jesuit system.

During the mid-seventeenth century there were three primary forms of theatrical performances. Court performances, usually in the form of intermezzi and opera were popular from Vienna to Dresden, as Italianate court theatres had become extremely popular. Secondly, Jesuit schools had begun to use drama as a means to educate students both for doctrinal content and for oratorical style. Finally, English troupes, forbidden to perform in commonwealth England during the Puritan

---

[1] Gerald Gillespie, Ed. <u>German Theatre Before 1750</u> (New York: Continuum Press, 1992), p. xiv.

interregnum, began to tour throughout the region. Because they did not speak German, the troupes were required to utilize primarily nonverbal activities. This resulted in much low comedy, and due to the nature of the entertainments, clown characters became very popular. By the early eighteenth century most plays featured the character *Hanswurst*, a hybrid clown character developed from commedia dell'arte characters, the medieval fool, and other various clown sources. The domination of drama by low comedy and *Hanswurst* made for a very unsophisticated form of theatre and left German drama in a very low state.

Gottsched and Neuber - Early Reforms

The first important steps toward significant theatrical production were taken by Johann Gottsched and Johann and Caroline Neuber in the first half of the eighteenth century. Gottsched (1700-1766) was a Leipzig professor and playwright who wanted to promote the German language as a vehicle for academic writing. Many of his ideas were borne from the desire to reform the traditional German drama, which until then had been dominated by low comedies and farce. Influenced by French Neoclassicism, Gottsched felt that drama had to teach moral lessons, observe the unities, and that characters should observe strict decorum.[2] In 1730 he published his *Versuch einer kritischen Dichtkünst für die Deutschen* (Essay in German Critical Poetics) which became the first formal statement of the neoclassical ideal in the German language.[3] He adapted and translated several French Neoclassical dramas, later borrowing the form for his own dramatic works. Gottsched worked closely with Caroline Neuber (1697-1760), who had formed a company of actors in 1727. Together, they began a partnership that would last until 1739 and would significantly change the direction of German theatre.

---

[2] Marvin Carlson, Theories of Theatre (Ithaca, N.Y.: Cornell University Press, 1984), p. 165.
[3] F.J. Lamport, German Classical Drama (Cambridge: Cambridge University Press, 1990), p. 8.

Most important for this study is the fact that Neuber and Gottsched made the first significant attempt in the German speaking world to establish performance standards for a company of actors. Because of the demands of the classically based texts, Neuber and her actors engaged in a series of practices that were new to the Germanic region. Later, their practices became known as the "Leipzig School of Acting," the first of a series of styles of acting in the region. They implemented a lengthy rehearsal process and discouraged improvisation during performances. They also analyzed plays more closely and attempted to realistically portray the heroic characters demanded by the new scripts. Theatrical conventions, such as the monologue and asides were discouraged, and virtually deleted from the playscripts by Gottsched.[4] Previously, Gottsched had made attempts to eliminate the *Hanswurst* from scripts in order to elevate German drama to a higher level of sophistication. Though not completely successful, Gottsched at least diminished the importance of the clown and the reliance on low comedy. Finally, they provided simple scenery and more carefully detailed settings than had been previously utilized in the German court dramas. Gottsched examined classical oratory with his actors and, while not always successful in his attempts, was at least partially responsible for raising the level of linguistic expertise in German theatre. Though these practices can hardly be considered an organized system of actor training, they established artistic objectives and an organizational framework on which future companies and their leaders could build.

Konrad Ekhof and the Beginnings of Acting Theory

Several of Neuber's company members would later form their own acting troupes, thereby extending Neuber's influence across the Germanic region. Friedrich Schönemann (1740-1782) founded a company that toured throughout eastern

---

[4]Marvin Carlson, Theories of the Theatre (Ithaca, N.Y.: Cornell University Press, 1984), p. 166.

Germany. Comprising the Schönemann Company were some of the greatest actors of the eighteenth century German stage, including Sophie Schroeder, Konrad Ackermann, and Konrad Ekhof. Ekhof (1720-1778) eventually became the company's leading actor; but more importantly, he was instrumental in the foundation of the Schönemann academy, an academy in Schwerin for the training of actors. Unfortunately, very little is known about the activities of the Schönemann Academy.

The group organized itself as a lecture series to inquire into performance practices and portrayal of characters, to observe and discuss performances, to undertake additional rehearsal and work on running performances, and to learn through collective criticism.[5] Ekhof was the inspirational leader, but deliberately underplayed his role as the teacher. In one of his initial lectures, Ekhof stated that he did not consider himself solely a teacher, but was himself still a student.[6] Everyone in the Schönemann Academy was given a chance to state his opinion; thus the formation of one of the first true ensembles. Ekhof felt that his real duty was to "monitor rational discussions about the art of acting in general."[7] Through his lectures and writings Ekhof established a theoretical base for the academy and for the art of acting in Germany. In 1753 he wrote;

> Dramatic art is copying nature by art and coming so near up to it that semblance is taken for reality, or to represent things of the past as if they were just happening. In order to obtain some mastery of this art the following things are required: a vivid imagination, untiring application, and a never idle practice.[8]

Ekhof's approach was based in simplicity; and, contrary to the French propensity to "overdecorate" he felt that actors should search for a methodology that

---

[5] Ottoftitz Gaillard Die realistischen Traditionen derdeutschen Schauspielkunst (Berlin: Herausgegeben vom Zentralvorstand der Gewerkschaft Kunst in FDGB, 1952), p. 15.

[6] Ibid., 16.

[7] Ibid., p. 16.

[8] Konrad Ekhof, quoted by Toby Cole and Helen Krich Chinoy in Actors on Acting (New York: Crown Publishers, 1965), p. 235.

would allow them to see the "root cause of everything." Acting, in Ekhof's opinion, amounted to a photographic "mapping out of society."[9] Due to his efforts at the Schönemann Academy, Ekhof is considered Germany's first acting theorist as well as the "father of German Acting."[10] Though the school eventually lost its following, Ekhof's attempt is important as the first step in the establishment of a realistic school of acting in Germany.

The next major step was taken in 1767 with the establishment of the Hamburg National Theatre. Developed by Ekhof, Konrad Ackermann, and members of an acting company that Ackermann had founded in 1753, the Hamburg National Theatre was designed to promote "fine drama and acting."[11] Primarily, the company performed French neoclassical works in German translation; but a substantial portion of the repertoire was reserved for native German playwrights, including Johann Elias Schlegel, C. F. Gellert, and Gotthold Ephraim Lessing. Lessing, remembered as one of the eighteenth century's greatest playwrights, was also employed by the theatre as a salaried critic to help to improve both the literary and performance standards of the theatre. During this venture, Lessing wrote the essays collected under the title, Hamburg Dramaturgy, one of the most influential theoretical treatises of eighteenth century German theatre.

The Hamburg Dramaturgy - Lessing's Theoretical Statement

Lessing's treatise is not only useful as an example of eighteenth century German acting theory, it also allows the modern theatre scholar to gain insight into the expectations of actors from a learned professional such as Lessing. The

---

[9] Ottofritz Gaillard, The realistischen Traditionen der deutschen Schauspielkunst (Berlin: Herausgegeben vom Zentralvorstand der Gewerkschaft Kunst im FDGB, 1952), p. 16.

[10] Simon Williams, German Actors of the Eighteenth and Nineteenth Centuries (London : Greenwood Press, 1985), p. 23.

[11] Toby Cole and Helen Krich Chinoy Actors on Acting (New York: Crown Publishers, 1965), . 235.

Dramaturgy, initially published in 1767-1769 as a series in a journal sponsored by the Hamburg National Theatre, has been passed down to us in the form of one hundred and four separate articles, seven of which deal with the art of acting. As a whole, Lessing favored a more realistic approach to acting and rejected the minor reforms of Gottsched. Most of his writings were based on the acting approach of Ekhof, though he often fluctuated between French emotionalism and the rising anti-emotional movement.[12]

In the Dramaturgy, one of the initial concerns for Lessing is method of delivery. Article 3 deals with realistic delivery, in which the actor is asked to speak words; "so that they may not appear as a troublesome unburdening of memory, but as spontaneous promptings of the actual condition."[13] Later in the same article, he analyzes the process of feeling, and whether or not the actor should actually feel what he is portraying. Lessing points out; "The actor may really feel very much and still appear to have no feeling...it may be present where we do not recognize it, and we may fancy we recognize it where it does not exist."[14]

The emphasis on feeling and emotion was a by-product of the French dramas which were being performed and/or adapted, and the elocutionary demands of the "French School" of acting. The primary goal, however, was the outward portrayal of emotions, such as anger, fear, and happiness. Observation was the chief form of research for the actor, so that a truth of appearance was achieved and not necessarily a truth of feeling.

A third area of analysis in the Dramaturgy is that of gesticulation. Lessing follows the advice of Hamlet asking "that insignificant hand gestures be avoided," and notes that actors must observe moderation in movement even when the lines written by the poet indicate otherwise. Judging from his comments, hand and

---

[12] Marvin Carlson Theories of the Theatre (Ithaca, N.Y.: Cornell University Press, 1984), p. 170.
[13] Gotthold Ephraim Lessing, "Hamburg Dramaturgy" Actors on Acting, Cole and Chinoy, Eds., (New York: Crown Publishers, 1965), p. 243.
[14] Ibid, p. 243.

arm gestures during this period were rather elaborate and quite artificial. Above all, Lessing states that gestures should be "significant" and should "add emphasis to the main point that the actor is making," and that they should not be "decorations" for their own sake.[15]

It is important to note that Lessing's writings were largely prescriptive and not descriptive, except as far as they were descriptive of the practices of Ekhof and the few actors he coached. On the whole, Lessing's criticism was offensive to the actors of the Hamburg National Theatre and provoked much debate and argument from the members of the company.[16] However, it did raise questions concerning "truth" in acting and therefore paved the way for further developments.

Schroeder, Iffland and Devrient - Romantic Acting Styles

The Hamburg National Theatre eventually passed into the hands of Friedrich Ludwig Schroeder (1744-1816), considered by many to be the greatest actor ever to walk the German stage.[17] The son of Sophie Schroeder (actress in the Schönemann Company), Schroeder remained aloof from the Hamburg company members, touring in Vienna and the provinces until the death of Ackermann in 1771. At that point he took control of the theatre for what was to become the "most splendid period of Hamburg theatre history, earning world renown for his theatre and the Hamburg audiences."[18] Schroeder continued the reformations begun by Lessing, expanding the repertoire, and recognizing dramas of the English Renaissance, rather than French Neoclassical drama as the model for an indigenous German drama. Schroeder's influence on acting was even more important. For him the actor, not the

---

[15] Ibid, p. 24.

[16] Marvin Carlson, Theories of the Theatre (Ithaca, N.Y.: Cornell University Press, 1984), p. 170.

[17] Oscar Brockett, History of the Theatre, 5th Edition (Boston: Allyn and Bacon, 1992), p. 358.

[18] Simon Williams, German Actors of the Eighteenth and Nineteenth Centuries (London : Greenwood Press, 1985), p. 55.

playwright, was the center of the drama, and he insisted that if the audience left saying "the play was beautifully written," the actor had failed.[19] His approach paralleled that of Edmund Kean, to whom he is often compared. Schroeder felt that though the audience should be aware of the actor's transformation, the actor should always maintain an awareness of self. Additionally, Schroeder was apparently influenced by Diderot, as he asked that the actor "never forget himself," and that the art of acting "is debased when it is merely associated with the imitation of various models."[20] In order to assure this, Schroeder often insisted that passages in plays be rewritten in order to reflect the capabilities of the actor. Through his career Schroeder performed at least seven hundred roles and is known for creating the "Hamburg School of Acting."[21]

The late eighteenth century saw the formation of many state-supported theatres in Germany in the tradition of the Hamburg National Theatre. The first of these was founded in 1775 in Gotha by the remaining members of the Hamburg National Theatre. Other resident companies were formed in Vienna, Mannheim, Cologne, Mainz, Salzburg, Weimar, Passau, and Berlin. From the Gotha theatre would rise the next great German actor, August Wilhelm Iffland (1759 - 1814), who would carry forth the simplified realistic style of acting practiced by Ekhof. Iffland was important because he, like Ekhof, did a great deal to spread the new simplified style of acting across the Germanic region. He was able to achieve this because he traveled widely throughout Germany, performing as an actor, and later serving as director and *Intendant*, or producer, at many of the new national theatres. Through his efforts, Iffland became recognized as the leading actor of late Eighteenth Century Germany and also one of its leading playwrights, having written at least thirty-seven plays. During his stay at the Mannheim Court theatre (c. 1779 - 1796), Iffland was

---

[19] Ibid, p. 58.

[20] Ibid, p. 59.

[21] Toby Cole and Helen Krich Chinoy, <u>Actors on Acting</u> (New York: Crown Publishers, 1965), p. 256.

instrumental in cultivating the "Mannheim School of Acting," - a style which, through its greater simplicity and directness, was even more realistic than previous styles. Trained by Ekhof and influenced by the writings of Lessing, Iffland continued the systematic analysis of the art of acting begun by his mentors. In particular, Iffland felt that all art, especially a "living art" such as theatre, should reflect nature as completely as possible. He would later state, "In the whole of nature there is nowhere uniformity...nothing is inappropriate...nature and perfection are synonymous. Those who depict *human beings* are the great actors."[22]

Implicit in Iffland's comments is that all behavior, regardless of how crude or unstageworthy, was necessary to bring "life" to the stage. With Iffland's new approach, actions such as slouching, belching, and cursing were thought to be appropriate stage behavior. However, and probably as a reaction against the bombastic style of delivery which had previously dominated the French and German stage, Iffland believed that the actor should avoid too many uncontrolled outbursts. Like his teacher Ekhof, Iffland felt that even during the height of passion an actor should display restraint, thus presenting a more noble view of humanity. While this view is inconsistent with his advocation of the portrayal of truth as found in nature, it was helpful in relaxing the rigid standards and previous bombasity of French influenced acting. Iffland's style, like that of Schroeder, introduced Romanticism into German acting.

Artists of the Germanic region had shown their ability to present radical forms of theatrical art with the *Sturm und Drang* (Storm and Stress) movement during the late eighteenth century. Described by Oscar Brockett and others as formless rebellions against neoclassicism, the movement faded because there was no unifying factor or theme. Romanticism had a much longer life because of its stronger theoretical basis, therefore giving it a greater impact on German acting. Romantic

---

[22]Simon Williams, German Actors of the Eighteenth and Nineteenth Centuries (London : Greenwood Press, 1985), p. 30.

actors were noted for their unconventional performance style and refusal to adopt a strict code of behavior. Romanticists were more likely to "follow their own bent," and trust their inspiration, than attempt to appeal to the audiences' sense of rationality.[23]

Perhaps the most prolific actor of the Romantic style was Ludwig Devrient (1784-1832). Also compared with the great English romantic actor Edmund Kean, Devrient was known for his ability to create an original role and to take the audience outside their realm of comfort in his portrayal.[24] Devrient was especially noted for his portrayal of character roles, like Falstaff, Shylock, and King Lear, created solely from himself without regard for previous models. Utilizing a method of acting regarded as the antithesis of the Weimar school (discussed later in this chapter), he refused to stoop to mannerisms and vocal patterns, opting instead to formulate his own perception of what a role needed.[25] According to his nephew, Eduard, Ludwig Devrient's power on stage lay in the fact that he kept the audience guessing, and that his approach, contrary to Iffland's, was somewhere outside the rational mind.[26] A severe alcoholic, Devrient's career was cut short and much of his latter years were plagued by inconsistency due to sickness.

Johann Wolfgang von Goethe and the Weimar School

Attempts to establish a German acting tradition were also hampered by the lack of a consistent view as to what comprised good or bad acting. This was no more evident than in the training procedures of Johann Wolfgang von Goethe (1749-

---

[23]Edwin Duerr, The Length and Depth of Acting (New York : Holt, Rinehardt and Winston, 1962), p. 295.

[24]Simon Williams, German Actors of the Eighteenth and Nineteenth Centuries (London : Greenwood Press, 1985), p. 77.

[25]Ibid, p. 68.

[26]Eduard Devrient Geschichte der Deutschen Schauspielkunst, Vol III. (Leipzig : Weber, 1848), p. 185.

1832) and his work at the Duchy of Weimar. Although Goethe's literary contributions remain among the most respected in the history of the German language, his approach to acting was in direct contrast to the previous efforts by those seeking to establish a realistic, "non-decorative" acting approach. Unlike Ekhof and Iffland, who sought to recreate natural everyday behavior in the theatre, Goethe sought to create a sense of artificial beauty on the stage, thus teaching actors to move with grace and to speak in an elevated manner so as to avoid "vulgar actuality."[27] Goethe established a set of maxims entitled "Rules for the Actor" in 1803 which, because of the Goethe's esteem and reputation, were widely dispersed across Germany. Initially, Goethe hoped to reform the technical aspects of acting, demanding that actors speak with clear diction devoid of provincial accents.[28] He discussed virtually all areas of vocal production, including placement, rate of speech, pitch, and emphasis. Later, Goethe discussed interpretation, and the idea of self versus character. Goethe compared the actor to a piano which "does not disown its character" when played. The notable exception in Goethe's opinion was the *forte*, or *furioso* passages, which required the actor to transcend himself to a higher realm.[29] Gesticulation was the next area of inquiry of the "rules." Goethe asked that actors present nature "ideally," thereby uniting the true with the beautiful.[30] Next, he included several rules for blocking, such as minimal profile playing and turning ones' back to the audience. Perhaps the most awkward rules had to do with posture, as Goethe asked actors to stand

> ... erect, the chest up, the upper half of the arms to the elbows close to the body, the head turned slightly towards the person to whom one is speaking, yet so slightly that three quarters of the face is always turned towards the audience.[31]

---

[27] Johann Wolfgang von Goethe "Rules for Actors" Arthur Woehl, Trans., cited in <u>Actors on Acting</u>, Cole and Chinoy, Eds. (New York : Crown Publishers, 1965), p. 247.

[28] Ibid, p. 249.

[29] Ibid, p. 250.

[30] Ibid, p. 252.

[31] Ibid, p. 252.

This passage gives an illustration of the artificiality that plagued the staging in Weimar. Later rules discuss placement, decoration and bad habits to be avoided on stage. Although these rules promoted an externally based, artificial approach to performing, generally called the "Weimar School of Acting," they provided later teachers and practitioners with a performance style to react against.

Prior to the eighteenth century the status of actors and troupes of performers was basically the same as vagrants and common criminals. Citizens were commonly warned to avoid them and to lock their doors against them if approached after sunset.[32] It was not an easy life for actors, many of whom were forced to travel throughout the provinces with their performances in order to sustain a living. The obvious exception to these squalid conditions was the situation of the emerging star performer, who, with higher salaries and a choice of playing locales, maintained a higher standard of living. This was not the case, however, for the majority of actors who, like the public who attended the theatre, were uneducated and illiterate. The public theatre in pre-eighteenth century Germany, was regarded with contempt by the educated class, the aristocracy and the clergy.

With the construction of lavish state theatres and salaried acting companies, the status of the actor began to improve throughout the eighteenth century. Performers were able to stay in one place for longer periods of time, thereby enabling them to establish themselves within communities. Managers of companies encouraged company members to be active in their cities in a positive manner, and stressed high moral character from the actors. One producer, Baron Herbert von Dalberg, *Intendant* of the Mannheim Court Theatre, created the possibility of life-long employment for certain actors and a pension after their retirement.[33] All in all the

---

[32]Bruce Matley, "A Description and Evaluation of Professional Actor Training in the West German Public Acting Schools of Hannover and Essen." Ph.D. Dissertation, Wayne State University, 1978,
[33]Ibid., p. 61.

Eduard Devrient (1801-1877)

Having been born into what was arguably the most famous acting family in German stage history, Eduard Devrient was placed on stage at a very early age, but did not study acting formally until his thirty-eighth year. Because of his family name and reputation, Devrient was allowed to study at the *Conservatoire* of the *Comedie Française* in 1839 for a period of one year. During that year, Devrient began to formulate principles for acting and also for the development of a school of acting. A year later, in 1840, Devrient published "*Über Theatreschule*," a utopian view of the process of training stage performers. Devrient's treatise would eventually influence some of the great acting schools of the twentieth century, primarily Reinhardt's *Schauspielschule des Deutschen Theaters*. In his treatise, Devrient called for state support of actors and theatre training programs. He stated, "Architecture, painting and music [students] are taken care of, but in the middle of all this the actor stands alone, and must grow in the wild."[34] Devrient was given the opportunity to test his ideas in 1844, when he was appointed director of the court theatre in Dresden. Though he was not afforded the ideal situation about which he had written, he was able to undertake the training of new performers for the company. Initially, he felt that the actor should be taught a type of body consciousness before being permitted to express the "atmosphere of a soul."[35] Devrient advocated training in voice and speech to provide a style of delivery that was full of expression, yet not forced like the elevated "storm of passion" taught by the French schools.[36] Most of Devrient's

---

[34]Eduard Devrient, Geschichte der deutschen Schauspielkunst, Vol. IV. (Leipzig : Weber, 1848), p.327.
[35]Ibid., p. 328.
[36]Ibid., p. 328.

theories can be traced back to those of Ekhof, in that he advocated a high degree of naturalness as opposed to the antiquated mannerisms of the Weimar School. Much bad acting, Devrient felt, was the public's fault; they expected a type of behavior on the stage that was not natural at all. Subtleness was more compelling for Devrient, who felt that "the calmest speech is immediately couched in the strongest tones."[37] His ideas extended to the arts of stage and costume design, as he decreed that all elements of the stage should appear unadorned and unforced.

In 1852 Devrient was appointed director of the *Karlsruhe Theater*, where he served for seventeen years. During this time and after his retirement, Devrient turned more to writing. In 1874 he published the definitive work on the history of German Acting to the year 1850. <u>Geschichte der Deutschen Schauspielkunst</u>, a mammoth five volume set, serves as testimony to Devrient's reverence for the art of acting.

Schreyvogel and Saxe-Meiningen: The Ensemble Approach

By the end of the eighteenth century German theatre had begun to evidence a growing sophistication. With the growth of resident companies, performance aesthetics as well as the level of acting prowess had become more refined. This, in turn, had paved the way for the in-depth analysis into the art of acting by Ekhof, Lessing and others. As a real acting tradition began to develop, this tradition could be passed on to others; thus, the formation of schools of acting. However, in Germany this was still a few years in coming. Most of the education of actors had been handled by private instruction and through apprenticeships with the acting companies. There had been a few sporadic attempts, such as the Schönemann

---

[37]Eduard Devrient, "Simplicity and Convention" <u>Actors on Acting</u>, Toby Cole and Helen Krich Chinoy Eds. (New York : Crown Publishers, 1965), p. 262.

Academy and the Hamburg National Theatre, but nothing as sustained as the *Conservatoire* of the *Comédie Française*.

With the development of national theatres, the emphasis shifted from individual performances and approaches to acting, to the formation of strong ensemble-based resident companies. The companies could then guarantee themselves a supply of performers by recruiting and training their own young actors. Several companies have already been mentioned but none was more important than the Vienna *Burgtheater*. Under the direct supervision of the Habsburg Court and the Emperor Josef II (1733 - 1817), the *Burgtheater* was fully subsidized by the court with its purpose being "to refine the taste and further the education of the audiences...appealing to the rational sentiments and perceptions of the audience members".[38] The daily affairs of the company were overseen by a board of senior company members, known as the *Ausschuss*. Primarily, the *Ausschuss* was concerned with the performance standards of the Viennese actors and their position in society.[39] As a member of the company, Friedrich Schroeder was influential in the development of the realistic style of acting engendered by the *Burgtheater*, and was elected to the *Ausschuss* in 1781. The company's most important period of artistic achievement came under the direction of Josef Schreyvogel (1768 - 1832), secretary of the theatre and also a free-lance art dealer and theatre critic during the early nineteenth century. Schreyvogel worked to establish a sense of nationalism within the company's repertoire by including important plays from all periods of dramatic literature. Additionally, a large number of plays from German authors were included to help define the company within its native culture. Schreyvogel's suggested repertoire has

---

[38] Simon Williams, German Actors of the Eighteenth and Nineteenth Centuries (London : Greenwood Press, 1985), p. 114.
[39] Ibid., p. 114.

served as a model for many of the world's best national theatres from his time until the present.[40]

Perhaps the most important contribution by Josef Schreyvogel was his emphasis on ensemble. According to Schreyvogel the play, not the actor, should be of primary importance, and all elements of the performance should support the whole. This was in contrast to the focus of most of the state-supported theatres in the Germanic Region, which had carried on the practice of hiring stars such as Iffland, Schroeder, and Ludwig Devrient. Instead of creating a venue for stars, Schreyvogel assembled a company of many different and varying types of actors who were flexible in the kind of characters that they could play. He was also instrumental in the development of an idealist form of acting, combining the formality of the Weimar School with the realism of the Mannheim school.[41] The resultant acting style was more intimate, largely due to the relative closeness of the actors to the audience at the *Burgtheater*.[42] Actors were able to underplay their lines instead of ranting and railing to reach the upper balcony. The result: a closer rapport between actor and spectator.

Possibly the strongest influence on German performance, acting, and theatre companies of the nineteenth century was to come from Georg II, Duke of Saxe-Meiningen (1826 - 1914). The practices of the Meiningen Players established a model for realistic theatrical production that greatly surpassed all prior efforts in Germany as well as the continent of Europe. The Duke delved into every detail of a script before beginning work on it, performing extensive research into the areas of settings and costumes - favoring historical accuracy over generalization. Detailed drawings were provided for sets and costumes, and he often traveled to other

---

[40] Ibid., p. 115.

[41] Ibid., p. 116.

[42] The Vienna *Burgtheater* has an extended forestage, shortened pit, and additional levels of gallery seating, therefore actors are virtually surrounded by spectators. Information on the *Burgtheater* is found in Smekal, Das Alte Burgtheater, Vienna, 1916, and in Alfred J. Loup "Vienna's *Burgtheater* in the 1970s Theatre Journal 32:1 (March 1980), p. 55-70.

countries to acquire the necessary visual insight or materials with which to work. Settings were authentic reproductions of Rome, the city of Thebes, or Lear's Castle.

In 1870 the Duke appointed Ludwig Chronegk (1837 - 1891) as director of the company. Chronegk, an accomplished comedic actor, taught the company members much about the association of movement on stage with the audiences' perception of their intended meaning.[43] Gesticulation was analyzed in terms of its function, and not as decoration or to achieve a particular effect. Both Chronegk and the Duke were particularly concerned with the details of crowd scenes, assigning each member of the chorus specific lines and duties. Instead of working with the chorus *en mass*, they divided the chorus into smaller groupings, each under the direction of an experienced actor. The smaller groups would then rehearse specific movements and lines before joining with the other groups. As a result, crowd scenes in Saxe-Meiningen's productions were characterized by individualization and particularization rather than generic uniformity. Rehearsals lasted for months, as each play was not opened "until it was ready."[44]

Chronegk and the Duke also extended their reforms to the behavior of performers, resulting in a company that was a true ensemble. They began by forbidding actors and actresses to tamper with their costumes, a practice that was common in the years before them. During the initial stages of rehearsal, each performer was provided with a costume design that he or she was expected to adhere to throughout the run of the performance. Furthermore, each member not cast in a major role was required to appear in the chorus and treat it as seriously as a leading part. Though not specifically an actor training program, the reforms of Saxe-Meiningen were extremely influential on later training programs, foremost among them the work of Konstantin Stanislavski.[45]

---

[43] Edwin Duerr, The Length and Depth of Acting (New York: Crown Publishers, 1954), p. 366.
[44] Ibid., p. 367.

[45] Toby Cole and Helen Krich Chinoy Actors on Acting (New York: Crown Publishers, 1965), p. 264.

Development of Acting Styles in Twentieth Century Germany

The preceding section has shown the fluctuation of German acting styles, moving from primitive attempts at realism, to romanticism, classicism, and finally back to realism. In the twentieth century a similar conglomeration of styles, methods of training actors and personalities is evident.

The first major influence on German acting in the twentieth century was Otto Brahm (1855 - 1912). A proponent of naturalism, Brahm founded the *Freie Bühne*[46] in 1889, which became Germany's most significant example of the Independent Theater Movement. Under Brahm's leadership, the *Freie Bühne* was organized as a private theatre devoted to the production of new naturalistic works by writers such as Ibsen, Hauptmann, and Gorki. The emphasis of the *Freie Bühne* was to present "human beings" on stage, with "a simple, natural voice, regardless of whether or not it was beautiful."[47] Plays were presented in a strikingly realistic manner, and in production offered an intimate observation of nature, which questioned the social standards of the time.[48]

Due largely to his success at the Freie Bühne, Brahm was appointed head of the *Deutsches Theater* in 1894 and together with Emmanuel Reichter, encouraged a new style of acting to compliment the naturalistic dramas. Initially his goal was to reform productions of the classics by employing the then-revolutionary naturalistic style of acting. Brahm was critical of classical, stylized forms of acting like that encouraged by Goethe, which was still practiced in German theatre. He asked that the actor rid himself of elevated speech and arbitrary mannerisms, opting instead to "speak in the living speech of our time and quicken old sluggish forms with powerful

---

[46] Literally the "Free Stage," the *Freie Bühne* was located at the Lessing Theatre in Berlin. Dates of the *Freie Bühne* were 1889 - 1894.
[47] Otto Brahm, "In Defense of Naturalism" <u>Actors on Acting</u>, Eds. Toby Cole and Helen Krich Chinoy (New York : Crown Publishers, 1965), p. 268.
[48] Marvin Carlson, <u>Theories of the Theatre</u> (Ithaca, N.Y. : Cornell University Press, 1984), P. 265.

modern feeling."[49] Like the great German Romanticists, Brahm asked that the actor imitate not ideal beauty, but reality, warts and all.

Although his style of production worked for many of the naturalistic dramas, Brahm's innovations did not mesh well with classical theatre, including the plays of Goethe, Schiller, and Lessing, which were often included in the repertory of the *Deutsches Theater*. Brahm's innovations were important as far as the development of the realistic movement is concerned; but much of the requisite theatricality was drained from his productions of classics. Eventually, Brahm began to offer fewer classical and nonrealistic plays at the *Deutsches Theater*, a policy which brought about severe criticism.[50] Brahm remained at the *Deutsches Theater* for ten years, retiring in 1904.

For some, the naturalistic period represented a low state in German theatre. Certainly no one was more vocal about his distaste for naturalism than Max Reinhardt (1873 - 1943). His work will be analyzed at greater length in the next chapter. Reinhardt's reactions against Brahm's decidedly naturalistic approach were instrumental in the re-theatricalization of theatre, and in the cultivation of an eclectic approach to directing, one in which each play was carefully analyzed and given its own style of production. Of significance for this study is the fact that Reinhardt established a school for acting at the *Deutsches Theater*. *The Schauspielschule des Deutschen Theaters* was founded as a private acting school in 1905 and continued through World War II. Reinhardt remained at the *Deutsches Theater* until 1933, when the rise of Hitler necessitated his departure.

Several other theatre schools were established during the early twentieth century. Included among those were the *Hochschule für Bühnenkunst "Louise Dumont"* (1904) in Düsseldorf, The *Schauspielschule der Vereinigten Stadttheater*

---

[49] Otto Brahm, "In Defense of Naturalism: Actors on Acting, Eds. Toby Cole and Helen Krich Chinoy (New York : Crown Publishers, 1965), p. 272.

[50] Edwin Duerr, The Length and Depth of Acting (New York : Holt, Rinehardt and Winston, 1962), p. 376.

Köln (1905), the *Frankfurt Schauspielschule* (1919), the *Städtische Schauspielschule Leipzig* (1921), and the *Theaterakademie Karlsruhe* (1927). Only the Leipzig school was state subsidized, making it the first state theatre school in Germany. Later, in 1922, the *Universität Jena* instituted a technical curriculum for the instruction of acting.[51] This model of technical instruction for actors provided by private or state funded academies would be the pervasive form of actor training from its inception to the present.

Antirealistic Acting

German drama between the wars included a number of theatrical genres. One movement that provided a different approach to the art of acting was Expressionism. Characterized by distortion, mechanization, and horror, expressionist dramas were popular in Germany between 1916 and 1924. Though it was a short-lived movement, it was extremely influential as far as the direction of German theatre was concerned.

Certainly the most important theories of acting, as far as expressionism is concerned, are those written by Paul Kornfield (1889 - 1944). A Czech-born dramatist, Kornfield completely renounced both naturalistic and classical styles of acting, favoring instead a pre-Brechtian, theatrically conscious form of acting. Kornfield scorned natural behavior, spontaneity, and reality of emotions. Instead of isolating particular traits of human behavior, and making efforts to faithfully copy them, Kornfield suggested:

> ...if the actor builds his characters from his experience of the emotion or fate he has to portray and with gestures adequate to this experience, and not from his recollections...he will see that his expression of a feeling that is not genuine and which has been artificially stimulated is purer, clearer, and stronger than that of

---

[51] Gerhard Ebert, Schauspieler Werden in Berlin (Berlin: Berlin Information, 1989), p. 27.

any person whose feeling is prompted by genuine stimulus.[52]

Actors were asked to forget their ties to everyday living, and behavior was modified to suit the "mechanization" and distortion of the scripts. Thus, actors were asked to chant or intone their lines, giving more weight to the sounds of the words than to their meaning.[53] The goal was to achieve a direct connection to the spectators' emotions as opposed to providing them with rational experience.

Another proponent of expressionist acting was Leopold Jessner (1878 - 1945). Jessner was in a better position than Kornfield to implement his expressionistic theories because of his appointment as *Intendant* of the *Berlin Staatstheater* (Berlin State Theatre), also known as the *Schauspielhaus*, in 1919. In addition, Jessner was appointed leader of the *Staatliche Schauspielschule Berlin*[54] in October 1925. The *Staatliche Schauspielschule* was the first state supported acting school in Berlin, and one of two state acting schools established in the early 1920's (the other in Leipzig). Education lasted two years, and was given in the areas of *sprechlehre* (speech training), *sprachliche stillehre* (speech styles), *fremdsprache* (foreign language), *körperliche ausbildung* (body/physical training), *gehörbildung* (ear training for music), *rollenstudium* (role study), *ensemblestudium* (ensemble performance) and *theatrewissenschaft* (theatre science). The program was short-lived, in comparison with the Reinhardt school and others, and was discontinued after World War II.

---

[52] Paul Kornfield, "Epilogue to the Actor" Anthology of German Expressionist Drama, Walter Sokel, Ed. (Ithaca, N.Y. : Cornell University Press, 1984), p. 7.

[53] Edwin Duerr, The Length and Depth of Acting (New York : Holt, Rinehardt and Winston, 1962), p. 439.

[54] There is no relationship between this school and the *Staatliche Schauspielschule Berlin*, founded in 1951 by the German Democratic Republic. The term literally means "State Acting School of Berlin" and has evidently been used twice in the history of German theatre education. The *Staatliche Schauspielschule* referenced here was taken over by the Nazis and the program was not continued after World War II.

Jessner proposed a "technique of signification," in which actors utilized only those details which would portray vital experience. Jessner encouraged actors to speak against their natural rhythm, with an intensity and rhythm that would electrify the audience. Influenced by Appia, Jessner believed that spatial arrangement on stage was an extremely important part of the audiences' perception of theatre. He believed that the actors should speak directly to the audience, and through their movements, along with the setting and lights, provide an experience that was not in any way a reproduction of life.[55]

Greater emphasis on political consciousness and the proletariat was seen in the work of Erwin Piscator (1893-1966). Piscator felt that the theatre had to address the larger problems of humanity to be effective, and that theatre should be used to promote the sociological revolution. Theatrical technology was also advanced by Piscator, whose use of complex stage machinery, slides and film created a new technical language for the stage. In Piscator's theatre the stage settings became an integral, changing component of the play's action. These innovations would later be grouped under the general heading of epic theatre.

To complement the epic theatrical style, Piscator also proposed a new form of acting which,

> ...estranges the events being presented on the stage from the spectator and makes the audience assume an inquiring and critical attitude....I cannot accept the Chekovian actor hypnotizing himself behind the fourth wall.[56]

Much of the impetus for this type of acting amounted to a clean break with the excesses of Expressionist acting. On the stage of the epic theatre, the actor was only one of many tools to be utilized in presenting the political message. Piscator proposed a cool, reserved approach to acting which de-emphasized

---

[55]Edwin Duerr, The Length and Depth of Acting (New York : Holt, Rinehardt and Winston, 1962), p. 441.

[56]Erwin Piscator, "Objective Acting" Actors on Acting. Toby Cole and Helen Krich Chinoy, Eds. (New York: Crown Publishers, 1965), p. 286.

the importance of the individual. Actors were encouraged to resist impulse and instinct, and to use their intellect to "reason out every movement."[57] Lines were spoken with little emphasis on the emotional content, and movement on the stage was subordinated to the overall *mise en scene*. In order to accomplish this, Piscator employed actual working-class citizens and amateur actors in his early productions, turning to professionals only after he had achieved commercial success.

Bertolt Brecht (1898 - 1956) was greatly influenced by Piscator's theatre, and adapted the epic model for his own use. However, while Piscator chose to emphasize the use of stage machinery and technical elements, Brecht preferred to explore the dialectical process through the play's content in addition to utilizing epic scenography.[58] Brecht adopted for his own use the process of *verfremdungseffekt* (distancing or alienation), initially conceived by Piscator. Brecht described alienation in the following way:

> To alienate an incident or character means simply to remove from the incident or character all that is taken for granted, all that is well known and generally accepted and to generate surprise and curiosity about them.[59]

In order to achieve this, Brecht developed an array of performance techniques. Brecht advised actors not to impersonate characters or attempt to live the part as with Stanislavskian acting, but to illustrate the behavior of a type of person in a particular situation. Actors were told to stand outside the characters they were playing and comment on them, using their powers of observation, and relating to the audience what their characters did. In the initial phases of rehearsal Brecht would occasionally

---

[57] Edwin Duerr The Length and Depth of Acting (New York : Holt, Rinehardt and Winston, 1962), p. 458.

[58] Michael Patterson, The Revolution in German Theatre 1900 - 1933 (London : Routledge & Kegan Paul, 1981), p. 154.

[59] Bertolt Brecht, Brecht on Theatre, translator and editor John Willett (London : Methuen, 1964), p. 136.

make actors speak lines in the third person, actually adding phrases such as "he said," or "she yelled," in addition to speaking the stage directions out loud. Dialogue was to be delivered in a "reporting" manner, instead of realistic exchange between characters. Above all, these techniques were to be executed without the use of stylized mannerisms. The Brecht actor should appear as a real person who is presenting a character in a play.

Another of the methods utilized by Brecht to alienate was the process of historicization, or placing events in the past, chronologically distancing them from the spectator's realm of experience. Therefore the historical parameters became equally as important as the actual occurrences, so the spectator would say "that's how I would act, if I had lived under those circumstances."[60]

Brecht was also instrumental in providing the art of German acting with one of its integral concepts - the concept of *Gestus*. *Gestus* is defined by Brecht as the realm of attitudes adopted by characters toward one another.[61] Each scene has a basic *Gest*; likewise, each character has a social *Gest*, with all incidents evolving from this basic *Gest*. Therefore a character's physical attitude and facial expression were influenced by his/her social *Gest*. The concept of *Gestus* extended into the realm of language, as the character's rhythm of speech and tone of voice were determined by *Gestus*.

Brecht's influence on contemporary German actor is equaled only by that of Russian actor/director Konstantin Stanislavski (1863 - 1938), who will be examined later. Stanislavski's system was adopted as the model for many German schools of acting which were developed in the early twentieth century, several of which will be discussed later in this study. Study of both Brecht and Stanislavski pervade the German theatre training system.

---

[60]John Rouse, Brecht and the West German Theatre (Ann Arbor, Michigan : University of Michigan Press, 1989), p. 28.
[61]Ibid, p. 198.

CHAPTER 2

MAX REINHARDT AND THE SCHAUSPIELSCHULE DES DEUTSCHEN THEATERS

Max Reinhardt

Before coming to Berlin in 1894, Max Reinhardt had studied acting privately and worked successfully as an actor in Salzburg, Austria. Otto Brahm, the *Intendant* of the *Deutsches Theater*, had seen Reinhardt during his early years at the Salzburg Town Theater, where the young Reinhardt had specialized in playing "old man" roles. This excited Brahm, who felt that there was a wide range of casting possibilities at the *Deutsches Theater* for the actor. Brahm invited Reinhardt to Berlin, to join the *Deutsches Theater* as a full company member.

During the early stages of his acting career at the *Deutsches Theater*, Reinhardt played leading roles such as Mephistopheles in Doctor Faustus and Puck in A Midsummer Night's Dream. However Brahm's decidedly naturalistic approach, which focused on the minute details of everyday life, did not satisfy Reinhardt's need for a "deep and pure spiritual art."[1] Reinhardt became frustrated with the situation at the *Deutsches Theater* and began to search for a medium through which he could experience greater creative pleasure. In 1898 be wrote in his diary "what I really want is to found an experimental stage for actors."[2] Two years later, in 1900, his dream was finally realized as he initiated a cabaret theatre called *Schall und Rauch* (Sound

---

[1] Gerhard Ebert, Schauspieler Werden in Berlin (Berlin: Berlini-Information, 1987), p.16.
[2] Max Reinhardt Schriften (Berlin: Hugo Fetting, 1974), p. 70.

and Smoke) for after-hours performances. This provided Reinhardt with a setting where he could experiment with concepts like actor/audience "communion," and his efforts to develop "a higher form of truth than naturalism could afford."[3] Located in a tiny rehearsal hall inside the *Deutsches Theater*, Reinhardt's company offered new and classical plays, original sketches, and other miscellaneous works. In 1902 his cabaret theater was relocated to an alternate site and was renamed the *Kleines Theater*, where Reinhardt presented new, more controversial works such as Wilde's Salome and Wedekind's Earth Spirit. In 1903 he left Brahm and the *Deutsches Theater* in order to concentrate completely on his producing and directing efforts.

During the next two years, Reinhardt worked primarily at two theatres: the *Kleines Theater*, where he continued his cabaret and chamber performances and the *Neues Theater*, a larger theatre space that could accommodate works on a grander scale.[4] At the *Neues Theater* he focused primarily on classical works, presenting Shakespeare's A Midsummer Night's Dream, Euripides' Medea, and Maeterlinck's Pelleas and Melisande.

Given the freedom and control that his ambition required, Reinhardt began to formulate theories of the theatre that would remain with him throughout his career. In a letter to his friend, Bertold Held, he stated, "What I want is a theatre, that once again gives the people joy, that can take them out of their gray misery of everyday and carry them out in a clean and pure air of beauty."[5] In short, Reinhardt was interested in re-theatricalizing the theatre. He was able to begin the implementation of this process in 1905, being appointed artistic director of the *Deutsches Theater* by the theatre's owner, Adolf L'Arronge, upon Brahm's retirement. One of his first goals was to create a stronger ensemble of actors, thereby influencing his decision to establish a school for acting. The *Schauspielschule des Deutschen*

---

[3] Gerhardt Ebert, Schauspieler Werden in Berlin (Berlin: Berlin-Information, 1987), p. 17.
[4] Later became the *Theater am Schiffbauerdamm*, the eventual home of the *Berliner Ensemble*.
[5] Max Reinhardt, Schriften (Berlin: Hugo Fetting, 1974), p. 71.

Theaters, discussed in greater detail later in this chapter, opened in September, 1905. Reinhardt also felt that scenography at the *Deutsches Theater* had been lacking under Brahm's leadership, so he set out to hire designers with "strong creative imagination."[6] Among the designers he contracted during his tenure were the Norwegian painter Edward Munch, English director/designer Edward Gordon Craig, and German designer Ernst Stern. Reinhardt's adoption of a more abstract visual style quickly replaced the naturalistic sets designed under Brahm's regime. The prevailing look of productions at the *Deutsches Theater* took on a sense of impressionism.[7]

On the 19th of October, 1905, Reinhardt's first production as artistic director opened. Kathchen of Heilbron, by Heinrich von Kleist, was not very well received as critics felt that there were too many decorations, inconsistencies in performance, and "too many extras!"[8] However, Reinhardt's next production, Shakespeare's The Merchant of Venice, brought him his first real success. One critic in particular noted, "each performance, from the great tragic role to the servant was individually sculpted and worked out artistically. The concert of voices was almost musical harmony."[9]

With the success of the The Merchant of Venice and the control of one of Europe's best equipped theatres, Reinhardt began to realize many of his artistic dreams. During his second season at the *Deutsches Theater* he opened an additional stage, the *Kammerspiele*, a smaller, more intimate stage for realistic plays. With the opening of the second stage another goal of Reinhardt's had been brought to fruition:

> Two stages, next to one another, the large one for classical plays and a smaller one for modern works. With the configuration of two stages,

---

[6]Michael Patterson, The Revolution in German Theatre 1900 - 1933. (London: Routledge & Kegan Paul, 1981), p. 34.

[7]Ibid., p. 34.

[8]Gerhard Ebert, Schauspieler Werden in Berlin (Berlin: Berlin-Information, 1987), p. 27.

[9]Ibid., p. 24.

actors and students will be able to practice both kinds of theatre and not be locked in to one kind or another.[10]

In 1906, he directed, with the help of assistants, twenty-four productions between the two theatres, with styles ranging from fantastic, to expressionistic, to realistic. He continued as *Intendant* at the *Deutsches Theater* for the next several years, directing at least twenty productions between the two theatres yearly and offering regional tours of many shows. As Reinhardt's vision began to grow he became aware of the limitations of the *Deutsches Theater*, which seated only 1,000. He planned for a "Theatre of Five Thousand" allowing festival seating in the spirit of ancient Greek drama.[11] Reinhardt's dream was realized in September of 1910 with his production of Oedipus Rex, which he took to the *Circus Schumann* in Berlin. Reinhardt had the interior converted into a replica of a Greek Amphitheater, complete with an orchestra, a gigantic permanent facade representing a palace, and seating on three sides of the action.[12] Utilizing his idea of theatre as a communal event, Reinhardt's conception of the play was "*Sprengung des Bühnenrahmens* " (lit. bursting the frame). He had the chorus mingle throughout the audience, with action taking place among the audience and as Reinhardt termed it, "playing out their drama in the midst of their fellow men, just as the great drama is played every day of our life on earth."[13] In keeping with his original intentions, Reinhardt created a modern equivalent for the original impact of Greek tragedy. He also established two interpenetrating realities - that of the audience and that of the on stage action.[14] The production was an international success, touring throughout Europe and the United Kingdom.

---

[10]Ibid., 24.

[11]J.L. Styan, Max Reinhardt (Cambridge: Cambridge University Press, 1982), p. 80.

[12]Douglas A. Russell, "The Visual Innovations of Max Reinhardt and His Designers," Modern Austrian Literature 18:2 (1985): 21-30.

[13]Huntly Carter, The Theatre of Max Reinhardt (New York: Bretano's, 1914), p. 210.

[14]Douglas A. Russell, "The Visual Innovations of Max Reinhardt and his Designers," Modern Austrian Literature 18.2 (1985), p. 24.

Reinhardt would stage hundreds of productions before presenting The Miracle in New York City over a decade later. His scenic designer for the production, Norman Bel Geddes, provides an excellent account of Reinhardt's directing approach in his text Miracle of the Evening, stating that Reinhardt was "the finest director I have ever seen."[15] Bel Geddes noted that Reinhardt's responsiveness to others placed them at ease, and whether the actor was third-rate or famous Reinhardt began by telling them that he would gladly welcome their interpretation of the part and adapt his own conception to theirs. By taking that approach, the actor was free to create and not imitate. Bel Geddes also noted that when an actor was having problems, Reinhardt would simply call him aside and make him aware of the limitations involved. Then he would make a few suggestions and help to get the actor back on track.[16]

Reinhardt retained his post at the *Deutsches Theater* until Hitler came to power in 1933. His association with the Salzburg Festival had brought him renown and directing opportunities in England and the United States as well as Munich, Austria, and other cities in Europe. He had a long and extremely prosperous career, directing over 970 productions in forty-two years (an average of 23.3 per year). When he departed Germany Reinhardt had directed and/or produced some 452 plays in Berlin alone - a total of 23, 374 performances. This amount is staggering, considering the number of plays he directed elsewhere.[17] Over the course of his career, Reinhardt directed productions in thirteen different countries, worked with some of the most accomplished actors of his day and had control of as many as five theatres simultaneously at several points during his career. Yet, perhaps his great directorial skill is best exemplified by the legacy of his *Regiebuch*, or working copy of the script complete with analysis, blocking, and designs completed prior to

---

[15] Norman Bell Geddes, Miracle in the Evening (New York: Doubleday & Company, 1960), p. 287.
[16] Ibid., p. 295.
[17] Oliver M. Sayler, Max Reinhardt and His Theatre (New York: Bretano's, 1924), p. 211.

beginning work on a production. Throughout his career Reinhardt formulated many more theories about acting than those he initially set forth. Before discussing his school of acting it will be useful to include some material which documents the basis of Reinhardt's theatrical theories.

Reinhardt's Theatrical Vision

A survey of Reinhardt's writings on theatre will immediately yield a variety of comments that deal in generalities and discuss theatre in terms of "broad strokes." Though most theatre historians are in agreement about Reinhardt's meticulous staging techniques for chorus scenes and the fact that he, like most German directors, was greatly influenced by the Duke of Saxe-Meiningen, extant interviews coupled with his own writings tend to be more vague than specific. Like most artists of his caliber, Reinhardt's ideas were often of monumental proportion and have been passed down almost in the form of edicts or maxims. Nevertheless, when combined with other sources, such as writings from students, colleagues, and actors with whom he worked, Reinhardt's dramatic technique can be seen with greater specificity.

After having taken control of the *Deutsches Theater*, Reinhardt's initial goal was to revive the theatricality of German acting and directing, which had been lost through the naturalistic movement. Reinhardt began with the premise that the first law of the theatre is simplicity - "the simplest forms, strong severe lines."[18] For Reinhardt, scenery and other accessories were, for the most part, superfluous; the only real decoration needed was lighting. In addition, Reinhardt established the appropriate spacial relationship between the actors and the spectators for each production. To achieve this he often attempted to recreate the original space for which the play was written. For example in 1910 for his production of Hamlet at the

---

[18] Huntly Carter, The Theatre of Max Reinhardt (New York: Bretano's, 1914), p. 122.

Deutsches Theater, he had several rows of seats removed and a forestage built in order to simulate an Elizabethan public stage. Later that same year he presented his previously mentioned production of Oedipus Rex at the *Circus Schumann* in Berlin, believing that Greek drama demanded a space much larger than the *Deutsches Theater*. For Reinhardt, no single approach was right for each play, and he made every effort to closely analyze and produce each play in a manner that would bring forth the essentials. He gave each play "it's individual style, it's own atmosphere, it's own music," and for this reason is often considered to be the first eclectic director.[19]

Because his productions were pared down to the essentials, actors were the primary focus. His most memorable productions were classical works, in which he utilized primarily two groups of performers - the chorus and principal performers. Reinhardt's work with the chorus is legendary. He made the chorus an integral part of his productions, choreographing their every movement and adding large sweeping unison gestures and patterns. In order for individual actors in Reinhardt's productions to maintain their balance against the chorus, they had to have an enormous level of personality and charisma.[20] This, therefore, was to become the focus of his actor training process: to raise the level of the actors performance personality and charisma through intensive vocal, physical, and emotional training.

Reinhardt's Work with Actors

As a prerequisite to studying with Reinhardt, an actor first had to pass Reinhardt's ultimate test: to convince the great master that he or she was completely committed to life in the theatre. Reinhardt was not willing to accept anyone who would not devote his or her entire time and energy to the art of the theatre:

---

[19]Ibid., p. 131.
[20]Ibid., p. 114.
[21]Ibid., p. 120

> ...the theatre only yields herself freely to those who entirely serve and worship her. He to whom the theatre is not the whole world, it's mirror and it's center has nothing to seek or gain therein. The theatre is a jealous goddess - she tolerates no other goddess, but she richly compensates him who devotes himself entirely to her.[21]

Once those few devoted individuals were selected, Reinhardt would invest his time in them. In the early stages of an aspiring artists' career, Reinhardt was careful not to try and impose qualities onto a theatre student, but to nurture and develop qualities which the student already possessed. According to Reinhardt:

> nature brings inexhaustible riches to no two creatures, and even the poorest has peculiarities which belong to him that are both full of charm and frightening.[22]

Believing that students should first learn themselves before attempting to portray others, Reinhardt focused the initial stages of training on the development of technical skills of speaking, singing, and movement. He warned them, "What you do not learn now, you will pay for later!"[23] Reinhardt worked with great diligence to make actors find feeling and gestures from within themselves, and not to resort to contrived poses and fabricated delivery. He did not believe that actors should wait until they got on stage to start speaking loudly and moving in an exaggerated manner. During the latter stages of an actors' training, he asked them to walk alone in the city or woods, using big gestures and loud delivery; in short, to begin to live in a manner that was broader and bigger than is usual. Reinhardt stated,

> I hate the actor that only becomes big on the stage and in the Inn...the theatre of today is not the world of appearances, but the world of being. You must be sincere and courageous with one another. This art is a

---

[22]Max Reinhardt, <u>Schriften</u> (Berlin: Hugo Fetting, 1974), p. 65.
[23]Gerhardt Ebert, <u>Schauspieler Werden in Berlin</u> (Berlin: Berlin-Information, 1987), p. 66.

> universal art, an ensemble art and only in ensemble...blossoms the unfading work of theatre.[24]

This indicates that Reinhardt intended to stretch them and make them larger than life, but in a manner that was not phony. He wanted actors to live everyday with the same energy as if they were on a stage. In keeping with his decision not to impose qualities on an actor, Reinhardt restrained from imposing his own will on student actors. This is a point of contention by many who have written about Reinhardt. Common opinion among theatre scholars in the United States for the past fifty years has been that Reinhardt contributed little to the art of acting due to his dictatorial nature;[25] but this is not the opinion of most German theatre scholars and practitioners. Those who know his work well draw a distinction between the way Reinhardt may have worked with a few "arrogant, untrained actors" and how he worked with students and actors who he trained.[26] With regard to particular choices about characterization, it was Reinhardt's goal to work with the actor and allow him/her to make original choices which were born from their own individuality. Primarily, he attempted to instill into the students one thing: confidence. Reinhardt felt that actors were instruments that come out of tune very easily and can give their best only when the strongest vitality and confidence is given them. According to Professor Wolfgang Rodler, Head of the Division of Acting at the *HfSK*,

> ...Reinhardt gave the actor freedom. He went into a rehearsal with a solid idea of what he wanted, but the actor would also come with ideas. So they would discuss the character and eventually both would take a detour in order to make it to the final destination. So you see, he employed an

---

[24]Max Reinhardt, Schriften (Berlin: Hugo Fetting, 1974), p. 322.
[25]This statement is based on comments which appear in Duerr's The Length and Depth of Acting and Matley's dissertation (see bibliography).
[26]Wolfgang Rodler, Berlin, Germany, May 1993.

indirect method, not through mandates or commands, but through suggestion and inspiration.[27]

Founding of the *Schauspielschule*

Having taken control of the *Deutsches Theater* in July, 1905, Reinhardt immediately made his intentions known to form a *Schauspielschule*, a school for acting. His official letter of intent, composed by his brother and legal council Edmund, read:

> To the *Konigliche Polizei-Prasidium* (Royal Legislative Commission).
> I would like to express the following: that I intend to found an acting school - the purpose being three-fold. To provide technical education to actors, to foster the study of both classical and modern drama, and to secure for my theatre a group of young recruits. The school, for which I have obtained a number of excellent faculty, could be opened by September.[28]

A month later he received a response:

> To Herr Director Max Reinhardt, in faithful response. With regard to your intention to found an acting school, the *Polizei-Prasidium* finds no objections to bring forth.[29]

Having been given the go ahead, Reinhardt acquired the *Palais Wesendock*, located near the *Deutsches Theater*. This building had a number of halls suitable for classrooms, as well as one large hall with a stage that could be used for master classes andperformances.Reinhardt was truthful in saying that he had assembled a number of excellent faculty. In the area of voice he had acquired Professor Emil Mann, a professor of Diction at *Berliner Universität*; Alexander Strakosch, one of Berlin's most famous speakers, as a voice and speech teacher; and Heinrich Laube, a well

---

[27] Wolfgang Rodler, Berlin, Germany, May 1993.

[28] Max Reinhardt, quoted in Gerhard Ebert, Schauspieler Werden in Berlin (Berlin: Berlin-Information, 1987), p. 10.

[29] Ibid., p. 10.

known actor and voice coach from Vienna's *Burgtheater*. Some of the teachers in the division of acting were Eduard von Winterstein, a famous German film actor, Bertold Held, Reinhardt's close friend and an actor from Salzburg and Gertrud Eyesoldt, one of Berlin's most successful stage actresses of the day.[30] Efraim Frisch, then a dramaturg at the *Deutsches Theater* under Reinhardt, was appointed as director of the school and would remain in this position for the next two years.

As is the case with most new artistic and/or academic ventures, the beginnings were not easy. Frisch made a mistake by accepting too many students - sixty - for the first class in September of 1905. This overage happened as a result of the relatively short time available to conduct auditions coupled with the number of promises made by Reinhardt and other members of the faculty to students and their families.[31] The large number of students made for many staffing problems - an average of twenty students in each improvisation class, and ten students in each voice class. Due to the nature of movement instruction, courses in fencing and stage movement were easier to handle. In order to subvert a disaster in the making, only twenty students were accepted into the 1906-1907 class.[32]

Students were granted admission by virtue of an audition and, in some ways more important, an interview with the staff, including Reinhardt. If accepted, the cost was six hundred marks yearly with no financial aid available.[33] If they elected to join the program, the students and their parents had to sign a legally binding contact stating that they would pay the required tuition. The school year consisted of two semesters, a fall term lasting from September 15 until December 1, and a winter

---

[30] Ibid., p. 27. No source was found to list the exact number of teachers at the *Schauspielschule des Deutschen Theaters*. Extant writings make mention of eight: five in acting and three in voice. Additional teachers not mentioned above are Hedwig Wangel and Albert Steinrück.

[31] Ibid., p. 27.

[32] Ibid., p. 27.

[33] This amount would be approximately six thousand *deutsche marks* by contemporary standards, so it was a moderately expensive school.

term lasting from February 15 until April 1. The training program lasted a period of two years.

During their first year of training, students were given only physical and vocal training, including stage diction, rhythmic movement, fencing, and a course in improvisation.[34] Not until the second year were the students given classes in "role study" (*rollenstudium*) and ensemble playing. Second year students were also required to present evenings of scenes, attended by the public. Unfortunately very little data exists which describes the content of these classes. Marlene Dietrich, who studied at the school in 1921-22 recalled, "We stood there mouthing vowel sounds into the vastness of the auditorium while tugging on ropes without gasping."[35]

Other published reports seem to indicate the intense psycho/spiritual nature of the acting classes with Reinhardt. Gertrud Eyesoldt, an instructor of acting stated,

> He lives in our blood, and deep is the contact between him and his actor. Yet only those who are true artists can own him. Weak talents dissolve him into an impersonal void. And he knows it. He instinctively seeks the artist. Whoever departs from him without any deep personal experience, has never sensed him.[36]

One aspect of the training program was the use of students to fill the large numbers of supernumeraries required by the productions at the *Deutsches Theater*. This situation, which received much attention by students, their families and professional actors at the *Deutsches Theater*, was viewed two ways. Initially, it was considered good, as it gave the students practical experience throughout their training and allowed them to make professional contacts. Increasingly, however, the stance was taken that the constant use of students in minor roles greatly hampered their

---

[34] Steven Bach, Marlene Dietrich: Life and Legend (New York: William Morrow & Company, 1992), p. 50.

[35] Ibid., p. 51.

[36] Oliver M. Sayler, Max Reinhardt and His Theatre (New York: Bretano's, 1924), p. 103.

training, since their participation in the productions took away from valuable class time.[37] It also brought about much harsh sentiment from professional actors, like the brochure distributed by Ernst Bergmann against the practices of Reinhardt. Written in 1906 and titled "The Fall of Reinhardt, or the Artistic Bankruptcy of the *Deutsches Theater*" (*Der Fall Reinhardt's Oder Der künstlerische Bankerott des Deutsches Theater*) the article was published in the form of a brochure and distributed by the disgruntled former actor. In it Bergmann claimed that Reinhardt could no longer afford real actors and was intending to put students on stage. The situation was embarrassing for Reinhardt initially, but Bergmann was finally quelled after being threatened with a lawsuit.[38]

While first year students were given close to six hours of instruction daily, second year students were seen "only once in a while at the school, and only if they were not needed in the theater."[39] Therefore, the reputation of the school had become that of an apprenticeship that one had to pay for. Another problem was the apparent lack of structure. Courses were outlined, but the nature of instruction varied, and course content was unpredictable. Because many of the instructors were professional actors or other theatre practitioners, they often had to miss class or arrange for substitutes in order to keep up with their own schedules. Despite this seeming plethora of problems, by 1910 the school had the reputation as one of Europe's best.[40]

The *Schauspielschule* 1910 - 1935

Because of his growing popularity in Germany, Europe and abroad,

---

[37] Gerhard Ebert, Schaupsieler Werden in Berlin (Berlin: Berlin-Information, 1987), p. 59.
[38] Ibid., p. 27.
[39] Ibid., p. 34.
[40] Steven Bach, Marlene Dietrich: Life and Legend (New York: William Morrow & Company, 1992), p. 48.

Reinhardt's involvement in the *Schauspielschule* began to diminish. Much restructuring had taken place, including an attempt, albeit unsuccessful, to arrange for state support for acting students.[41] Reinhardt had approached the *Oberpräsidium* (president or chairman) of the province of Brandenburg with his request, using Devrient's famous article "*Über Theaterschule*" as the basis of his argument. He complained of the lack of a German acting school on the same level with the *Conservatoire* of the *Comedie Francaise* and with the newly founded *Staatliche Schauspielschule Wien* (State Acting School of Vienna, later known as the Max-Reinhardt Seminar), both of which had secured state support.[42] The school had, for the most part, moved into the *Kammerspiele*, the smaller of the two stages which constituted the *Deutsches Theater*, and class sizes had become much smaller. Prior to 1911 the school had accepted between thirty and forty students per year. However, the move into the *Kammerspiele* combined with increasingly limited resources and the desire to ensure that each student receive an acceptable amount of individual instruction prompted the decision to accept only 6 to 8 students each year.

In 1914 the directorship of the school was passed over to Bertold Held, one of the school's original acting instructors and one of Reinhardt's closest friends. Paul Legband had served as school leader from 1907 until 1914, but during these early years the leadership of the school was not always clear.[43] Held had worked closely with Reinhardt on many productions, like the world famous Oedipus Rex at Berlin's *Circus Schumann*, helping the great director put the final touches on crowd scenes. However, Held was not very popular with the students, many of whom considered him arrogant. Marlene Dietrich, who studied under Held, regarded him

---

[41] Gerhard Ebert, Schauspieler Werden in Berlin (Berlin: Berlin-Information, 1987), p. 32.

[42] Reinhardt's request was denied, however a state school for acting was formed in 1925 in Berlin – the first *Staatliche Schauspielschule*.

[43] Gerhard Ebert, Schauspieler Werden in Berlin (Berlin: Berlin-Information, 1987), p. 37.

as a fool and an ineffective teacher whose pomposity was part of the price one had to pay to study there.[44]

During Held's tenure several official policies were instituted regarding the students work at the *Schauspielschule*. First, classes would be offered in the afternoons at the *Kammerspiele* rehearsal stage and at the *Palais Wesendock* with rehearsals for Deutsches Theater productions taking place in the mornings. Secondly, there would be one evening of scenes per month, performed by second year students to an invited public. Finally, Held approved of the continued use of students in the theatre's repertory productions. Students would work in all phases of the productions at the *Deutsches Theater*, and would be given first priority for small roles and supernumerary positions. Also instituted was a performance series in which the students could take leading roles. *"Bühne der Jugend"* (Stage of Youth) allowed for monthly performances which were attended by a paying audience and reviewers from several of the Berlin newspapers. Though few students could tolerate Held, his reforms standardized much of the practice at the *Schauspielschule*, which previously had been inconsistent and arbitrary.[45]

A number of German theatre schools were established during this period. In actuality, the Reinhardt School had been the third school established in the city of Berlin alone, with the *Marie-Seebach Schule* and the State *Hochschule* for Dramatic Art (*Reichersche Hochschule für dramatische Künst*) both opening in 1899. With the establishment of the Reinhardt School and its immediate attraction, the *Marie-Seebach Schule* began to lose its prominence and closed in 1922. The State *Hochschule* for Dramatic Art changed its curriculum, and began to focus on the training of opera singers.[46] Other schools were founded throughout Germany, perhaps the most prominent being the *Hochschule für Bühnenkunst Düsseldorf*,

---

[44]Steven Bach, Marlene Dietrich: Life and Legend (New York: William Morrow & Company, 1992), p. 51.
[45]Ibid., p. 52.
[46]Ibid., p. 32.

founded in 1904 by Louise Dumont, and the *Theaterakademie Karlsrühe*, which can be traced to the actor training work of Eduard Devrient, officially chartered in 1927. With no state subsidy, the Reinhardt School had to rely on three things in order to attract the best students: its relationship with the *Deutsches Theater*; keeping the best professors, including major Berlin actors and directors on staff; and maintaining its high profile and record of placement. From the outset Held had maintained that the school would not offer academic education, but purposeful training for future professional actors. Held stressed the training of the whole person, the command of all gestures, and the cultivation of a full range of emotions. Like his friend Reinhardt, he believed very strongly that the teacher should seek to develop the actor's inborn qualities, and that acting did not consist of disguise, but unveiling. Held remained at the *Schauspielschule* until 1931, the year of his death.

On the occasion of the twenty-fifth anniversary of the *Schauspielschule des Deutschen Theaters*, statistics were released regarding professional employment for graduates. From 1905 until 1930, six hundred and seventy students had graduated from the *Schauspielschule*. Of those, four hundred and fifty five had been accounted for. Two hundred of those accounted for were still working professionally in theatre and/or film. Ten members from the first class (1905) were still working in theatre.[47]

The *Schauspielschule* in the Third Reich

On January 30, 1933, Adolf Hitler became Chancellor of Germany. With the takeover of the Nazis, many theatre artists, including Reinhardt and Brecht, fled Germany. Reinhardt had designated Dr. Rudolf Beer and Karl-Heinz Martin to assume the leadership positions of the *Deutsches Theater* and the *Schauspielschule* respectively, but both men were removed by the Nazis and replaced by one man - Carl Ludwig Anchaz. Anchaz allowed Woldemar Runge, a Nazi supporter who had taken

---

[47]Ibid., p. 71.

Held's place in 1931, to retain his position as leader of the school.

While artistic suppression began almost immediately throughout Germany, activities at the *Schauspielschule* remained relatively unaffected until 1937. Initially, the Nazis cultural oversight committee, the Ministry of People's Instruction and Propaganda (*Reichsministerium für Volksaufklärung und Propaganda*), had accepted the basic idea of a realistic, Stanislavski-based approach to acting, and through their scrutiny, had designated the *Schauspielschule des Deutschen Theaters* as a model program.[48] However, around 1937 the cultural committee began to favor a different brand of emotional exploration, known as *Psychotechnik*. For this approach actors were forced to undergo intense emotional memory exercises, in order to present what proponents termed "a wider expressive range of emotions on stage."[49] The acting style that resulted has been described as indicative of the mixture of high energy, terror, and great depths of despair that accompanied Hitler's reign. The delivery which accompanied this approach shifted to a cold, ceremonious style, characteristic of Hitler's official announcements, and was named Reich-Chancellory-Style (*Reichkanzleistil*).[50] Several instructors from the *Schauspielschule* were removed and replaced with those more in line with the accepted approach. Hugo Werner-Kahle was installed by the *Reichministerium* as the leader of the school and Heinz Hilpert, Ernst Karchow, Dr. Wolfgang Drews, Bruno Hübner, Claus Clausen, Heinz Dieter Kentner and Margrit Glaser, all performers sympathetic to the Nazi cause, were placed at the school as instructors. Additionally, the school was granted a state subsidy by the *Reichsministerium*, which provided state funds for the operation of the *Schauspielschule* and subsidized tuition for all students. These funds, however, were conditional, based observance of the following stipulations: the *Reichstheaterkammer*

---

[48]Ibid., p. 89.

[49]Ibid., p. 87.

[50]John Rouse, <u>Brecht and the West German Theatre</u> (Ann Arbor: University of Michigan Press, 1989), p. 23

(theater chamber) retained the right to supervise all activities at the school; operating costs of the school were not to exceed 900 marks monthly; persons of non-Aryan descent could not be involved with the school, neither as teacher nor student; the *Reichsministerium* would examine all text books in use and replace them if necessary. Students were accepted into the *Schauspielschule* based on their physical attractiveness and approved racial characteristics.[51]

As the theatre became recognized as a valuable tool for the conveyance of propaganda, Joseph Goebbels took an active role in the direction of actor training. In June of 1938, Goebbels established a *Reichstheaterakademie* in Vienna, which would produce artists thoroughly in line with party ideology and committed to Nazi ideals. Goebbels also began to carefully scrutinize other theater academies with regard to their adherence to Nazi ideals. Among Goebbels' long range plans was the closing of both the *Schauspielschule des Deutschen Theaters* and the *Staatliche Schauspielschule*, replacing both with a single *Reichstheaterakademie Berlin*. The academy would be committed to, "Securing young recruits for the German stage who would be trained in the spirit of National Socialism."[52]

With the outbreak of war, Goebbels' plans were put on hold. Some reorganization took place at the *Schauspielschule*, with Willy Schürmann-Horster installed in 1941, for what would be a short tenure, as school leader. Schürmann-Horster proved to be less of a marionette than Goebbels had hoped by promoting such anti-Nazi ideals as independent thinking and the reading of plays and literature that had been disallowed. This provided Goebbels with the excuse he was looking for and the school was closed in 1943. The official statement read, "The School of the *Deutsches Theater* under Schürmann-Horster is a breeding ground for doubtful state political elements."[53] While plans were being made to transport several of the students

---

[51] Ibid., p. 87.

[52] Ibid., p. 90.

[53] Ibid., p. 94.

into a newly established School for actors and singers (*Schauspiel- und Sänger-Ausbildungsinstitute*) in Berlin, the fighting had become to heavy. All theatres were officially closed in 1944.

CHAPTER 3

DEVELOPMENT OF EAST GERMAN THEATRE AESTHETICS

The *Staatliche Schauspielschule Berlin* was established during the divided Germanys as one of the theatre training institutions of the German Democratic Republic. First, it must be understood that in the GDR theory and dogma were considered integral components of everyday life. In order to provide the reader with important background information concerning this phenomenon, this chapter will explore the theoretical basis of actor training in the former East Germany.

German Theatre After the War

During the latter stages of World War II and the period of recovery that followed, theatrical activity had been halted throughout most of Germany. In May 1945, theatres in Berlin were given permission to resume activity, but the severe damage incurred by many of them prohibited their opening until much later. The *Deutsches Theater* had suffered some damage and was unable to officially re-open on September 1945.[1] In the summer of 1945 training had resumed at the *Schauspielschule des Deutschen Theatres*. Hugo Werner-Kahle was re-appointed as leader of the *Schauspielschule*, but shortly thereafter was released due to his involvement with the Nazi party.[2] The leadership of the school was rather loosely

---

[1] Lessing's Nathan der Weise had played on September 7th, 1945. Prior to this two productions had played, Schiller's Parasit (June 26, 1945) and Thorton Wilder's Our Town, (August 3, 1945), but these performances utilized minimal settings and were scheduled around much of the salvage work.

[2] Gerhard Ebert, Schauspieler Werden in Berlin (Berlin: Berlin-Information, 1987), p. 98.

defined until September 1, 1946, when Wolfgang Langhoff took the position.[3]

Langhoff, then the *Intendant* of the *Deutsches Theater*, was in the position to exert an enormous amount of influence on the direction of theatre training in Berlin. Immediately, he wanted to restore the tradition of the school and to find a permanent location for the *Schauspielschule*. Langhoff then located several former teachers, familiar with the approach to acting which had been utilized prior to 1933, who had been released from the school by the Nazi authorities. During 1945 and 1946 classes had been conducted in a variety of locales, ranging from office suites of the destroyed *Schiller Theater* to available spaces in the *Kammerspiele* and *Deutsches Theater*. To provide a more stable setting, Langhoff secured locations for instruction in the Foyer of the *Deutsches Theater* and on Saarbrucker Street next to the theatre. Thirty new students were recruited and the program was completely revived. Given his duties as Intendant and director, Langhoff remained as director of the *Schauspielschule* just long enough for activities to become stabilized. Wolfgang Weyrach, a professor of acting, agreed to accept the responsibilities for a short time, with the bulk of major decisions and policies retained by Langhoff.[4]

The German Democratic Republic

After World War II, the country of Germany was divided into four zones, with one area each going to the British, American, French and Soviet Union. The German Democratic Republic, or East Germany, was established in 1949 in the area corresponding to the Soviet Occupational Zone. Although the Soviet Union did not pursue a rapid "Sovietization" of their area of occupation, there was almost immediately a different type of governmental structure set up by the Soviet Military

---

[3]Rudolf Hammacher and Gustav von Wangenheim took care of leadership responsibilities during that time.

[4]Gerhard Ebert, Schauspieler Werden in Berlin (Berlin: Berlin-Information, 1987), p. 106.

Authorities than that of the west.[5] On June 10, 1945, the Soviet Military Government issued the following statement:

> Within the territories of the Soviet Zone of Occupation in Germany, the formation and activity of all such anti-Fascist parties may be permitted which have as their aim the final eradication of all remnants of Fascism, the strengthening of the bases of democracy and civil rights in Germany and the development of initiative and self-sufficiency amongst the mass of people toward this end.[6]

After it's formation in October, 1949, the German Democratic Republic lasted for a period of forty years, until October 1989. During that span of four decades the country managed to amass a fairly large measure of international attention and notoriety; the GDR was denied entry into the United Nations until 1973 and had associated with countries thought to be unfriendly to the West, such as China and Cuba. East German sports teams dominated international competition, and in many events finished second only to the Soviet Union. The proximity of the German Democratic Republic to the newly formed Federal Republic of Germany created a mythical frontier on which it appeared that the final battle of capitalism and socialism would be fought. Karl Marx predicted that this battle was inevitable, and would undoubtedly be won by socialism. However, history proved Karl Marx wrong, and the German Democratic Republic was formally dismantled in 1989. From birth to death, citizens of the GDR were barraged by ideology and propaganda. Socialist ideology pervaded the country, molding the attitudes of the citizens and providing them with an inescapable awareness of their socialist lifestyle.[7] The official view of GDR citizens was that they were part of a natural progression in the triumph of socialism over capitalism, stemming from the feudal system in medieval times through

---

[5]Eberhard Schneider, The German Democratic Republic: The History, Politics, Economy, and Society of East Germany (New York: St. Martin's Press, 1978), p. viii.
[6]Kurt Sontheimer and Wilhelm Bleek, The Government and Politics of East Germany (London: St. Martin's Press, 1975), p. 27.
[7]Ibid., p. 37.

the temporary victory of capitalism and finally to the development of communism. Throughout the early years of the GDR and its constantly developing brand of socialism, the *SED* continued to be the mouthpiece for official policy and political matters. Through a series of annual conferences (discussed later in this chapter), the *SED* was responsible for the evolutionary process of defining what socialism meant for citizens of the GDR. The basic premises on which the society was built consisted of the Ten Socialist Commandments: 1. Always support the international solidarity of the working class and all working people, and the unbreakable bond between socialist nations; 2. Love your fatherland and always be prepared to use all of your strength and resources for the defense of the Worker's and Farmer's state; 3. Help to eradicate the exploitation of man by other men; 4. Do good deeds for socialism, because socialist leads to a better life for all working people; 5. To aid the development of socialism, always act in the spirit of mutual help and comradely cooperation, respect the collective, and welcome its criticism; 6. Defend and propagate the people's property; 7. Always strive to improve your achievements, be frugal and solidify the discipline of socialist work; 8. Raise your children in the spirit of peace and socialism so that they may become roundly educated human beings of strong character and bodies of steel; 9. Live cleanly and properly, respect your family; 10. Practice solidarity with those peoples fighting for national liberation and those defending their national independence.[8]

  Because art, literature, and drama were felt to be an important aspect of socialist society, many leaders of the German Democratic Republic felt that the Soviet model should be followed very closely, almost adhered to as a rule. This policy in itself created a battleground among German nationalists and those who sought to promote the Soviet model. Eventually there was some blending and the hybrid form that was developed would form the model for East Germany.

---

[8]The Ten Socialist Commandments, developed by Walter Ulbricht at the fifth Party Congress of the SED in 1958. Taken from H. G. Huettich, Theater in the Planned Society: Contemporary Drama in the German Democratic Republic. Chapel Hill: University of North Carolina Press, 1978.

Socialist Realism in the U.S.S.R.

Following the 1917 Revolution in the Soviet Union, the movement toward communism was swift. Power became increasingly centralized, and all areas of society were forced to conform to party ideology. Movements to control literature and the arts, though slow in coming, were finally necessary to curtail radical groups who interpreted Communism and Socialism in an unacceptable manner. The first steps were taken in 1925, as the Central Committee of the *Bolshevik* Party issued a statement "On Party Politics Concerning Imaginative Literature," emphasizing a new socialist literature.[9] Other steps were taken by the Russian Association of Proletarian Writers, which attempted to wipe out all bourgeois forms of art. In 1927 Stalin instituted his Five-Year Plan, which included measures for the reform of art in the Soviet Union. During this time it became necessary for the government to adopt strict parameters for the writing of literature and drama, since it had been decided that they should be used as vehicles for party ideology. These reforms gave birth to a body of literature which would become known as socialist realism - the officially sanctioned version of art and literature.

The concept of socialist realism was based on the writings of Lenin, Marx, and Engels, and proposed that literature and drama should advocate a positive view of socialist society, and to do so in a realistic style that was easily understood by the masses. Leading characters were those in support of the communist movement, and the antagonists were those who opposed it. For a play to have a happy ending, it should point to the ultimate triumph of communism over its enemies. Plays and novels were to include a *positiver held* (positive hero), who singularly embodied the ideas the author wished to convey. This hero would, after a series of conflicts, subordinate his desires and/or needs to the needs of society as a whole.

---

[9] George Bisztray, Marxist Models of Literary Realism (New York: Columbia University Press, 1978), p. 40.

The movement was strengthened with the formation of the Union of Soviet Writers in 1932, created to insure that literary and dramatic artists were ideologically correct in their attitudes toward socialist goals. Through Stalin's patronage they gained a great deal of power, and in 1934 at the First Soviet Writer's Conference policies were established that were to become the basis for socialist realist theory. Andrei Zhdanov, one of Stalin's chief cultural advisors and a member of the union, described the ideal Soviet Literature as; "A literature that defends and upholds the principle of equal rights for the workers of all nations, to abolish once and for all every kind of exploitation and the yoke of wage slavery."[10] Zhdanov's treatise discussed the growth and development of socialist literature and its impending domination over the literature of capitalist nations. As far as subject matter for socialist literature was concerned, Zhdanov described the characters in Soviet literature (including drama) as, "the active workers of a new life... comprising all walks of life including working men and women, collective farmers, engineers, business managers, and the like."[11] Above all Zhdanov pointed out that works of art should depict life truthfully, not in a dead scholarly way, not simply as objective reality, but to depict reality in its revolutionary development.[12] Socialist realism was seen as the natural progression of realistic art, which had outgrown idealistic and mystic tendencies. Nikolai Bukharin compared socialist realism to general realism saying;

> Socialist realism is distinguished from the other realism by the fact that it inevitably focuses attention on the portrayal of the building of socialism, the struggle of the new man, and all the manifold complexities of "connections and settings" of the great historical process of our day.[13]

---

[10] Andrei A. Zhadanov, "Soviet Literature - The Richest in Ideas, the Most Advanced Literature," in Dramatic Theory and Criticism: Greeks to Grotowski ed. Bernard Dukore (New York: Holt, Rinehardt and Winston, 1974), p. 960.

[11] Ibid., p. 960.

[12] Ibid., p. 961.

[13] Nikolai Bukharin, "Poetry, Politics, and the Problems of Poetry in the U.S.S.R." in Dramatic Theory and Criticism ed. Bernart Dukore (New York: Holt, Rinehardt and Winston, 1974), p. 968.

According to Bukharin, socialist realism conveyed real feelings and passions, and real history. More importantly, socialist realism pointed toward the future, to the establishment of new human qualities and the feeling of a collective bond between people.

Yet another view of socialist realism was provided at the Conference by Karl Radek. Like Bucharin, Radek's discussion compared socialist realism to general realism, with the key distinction being;

> Socialist realism means not only knowing reality as it is, but whither it is moving. It is moving towards socialism, it is moving toward the victory of the international proletariat. And a work of art created by a socialist realist is one which shows whither that conflict of contradictions is leading which the artist has seen is life and reflected in his work.[14]

Radek's main theme was that socialist realism should point to the decay of capitalism as a product of the past, a historical inevitability. Socialist realistic literature should allow man to look outside of himself, and begin the remolding process. Several years later, in 1946, at the annual meeting of the Central Committee of the Communist Party, another policy statement was released. Once again composed by Zhdanov, the statement read: Dramatic Literature and the theaters must reflect in plays and performances the life of Soviet society in its incessant surge forward, and contribute fully to the further development of the best sides of Soviet man's character which have been shown so patiently during the great fatherland war. Playwrights and directors must make Soviet youth spirited, optimistic, devoted to their community, believing in the victory of our cause, unafraid of obstacles, and capable of overcoming any difficulty. The theater must show that such qualities belong not only to a few select heroes but to many millions of Soviet citizens.[15] The Soviet model of socialism and the genre of Socialist Realism were both very important in East Germany, since

---

[14] Karl Radek, "Contemporary World Literature and the Tasks of Proletarian Art," in <u>Dramatic Theory and Criticism</u> ed. Bernard Dukore (New York: Holt, Rinehardt and Winston, 1974), p. 965.

[15] H.G. Huettich, <u>Theatre in the Planned Society: Contemporary Theatre in the German Democratic Republic</u> (Chapel Hill: University of North Carolina Press, 1978), p. 14.

together they provided the basis for the development of theatre aesthetics in the German Democratic Republic.

Development of East German Theatre Aesthetics

As a point of departure in discussing East German performance theory and/or performance aesthetics the theories and practice of Konstantin Stanislavski must be placed first, because Stanislavski's method and approach had Stalin's official sanction and would, therefore, be of primary importance in East German theatre aesthetics.[16] However, the work of Bertolt Brecht must also be considered, including the position of both Stanislavski and Brecht within socialist aesthetics. It is important to acknowledge the co-existence of the two ideologies within the East German theatre system, and the later theoretical works that evolved from this co-existence. Maxim Vallentin, Ottofritz Gaillard and Rudolf Penka, who were instrumental in the development and implementation of the Stanislavski and Brecht systems for acting in East Germany, fall into this category. Initially, however, the literary standards were of chief concern.

It was neither the desire of the German Democratic Republic nor of the Soviet Union that the GDR become an exact replica of the Soviet Union in its political and social development. Key to the formation of the GDR was the independent development of socialism, consistent with the theories of Lenin, Marx and Engels. From the outset it was felt that the construction of socialism in the GDR had the capability of being a model system, because of its proximity to both capitalist West Germany and the major communist countries of Eastern Europe. It was felt that the struggle between the two German systems would become a paradigm for the international struggle of socialism against capitalism.[17] However, with regard to art

---

[16]Ibid., p. 14.

[17]Kurt Sontheimer <u>The Government and Politics of East Germany</u> (London: St. Martin's Press, 1975), p.45.

and literature, the Soviet model was considered especially important as a theoretical base for the development of a body of socialist literature. The German Writers Conference of 1947 has been described in the following way;

> the cultural functionaries of East Berlin, reinforced by the large number of returned left-wing emigrants, grasped at the tradition of pre-1933, proletarian-oriented literature from the German revolutionary movement of the twenties, now officially referred to as "the Way," and tried to emulate in all cultural affairs the "great" and revolutionary example of the Soviet Union.[18]

Following the Soviet example, the political leaders of the *SED* developed a two-year plan at the First Party Conference of the *SED* in 1948 for the implementation of socialist realism. The objective of art, according to the *SED*, should be to educate people and lead them to a new social insight and a new relation to work. Formalism, art for art's sake, mysticism and the like was to have no place in socialist society. Art had to be realistic, party oriented and functional (i.e. educational). All areas of the educational system of the GDR, including the training of actors and other artists, were subject to close scrutiny by the Ministry of Popular Education and, in the case of the training of artists, the Ministry of Culture was also heavily involved. The cultural objective of the GDR, formulated at the First Party Conference of the *SED* in 1948 was:

> ...to educate people by way of a new social insight and a new relationship to work. This can only be achieved if all writers and artists dedicate their entire strength and enthusiasm to the task. The contribution of writers and artists toward the two-year plan consists of the development of realistic art, and the desire to reach the highest artistic achievements in their fields. Through their works, progressive writers can help to develop the joy of work and optimism of the workers in factories and the working rural population.[19]

Later, in 1963, after the 6th Party Conference of the *SED*, a law was passed which

---

[18] H.G. Huettich, Theatre in the Planned Society: Contemporary Theatre in the German Democratic Republic (Chapel Hill: University of North Carolina Press, 1978), p. 11.
[19] Ibid., p. 79.

standardized the socialist system of education (*bildungssystem*) for East Germany. Schools were designated as an instrument of the working class for the education and training of the growing generation."[20] The first strategic objective of the educational system of the GDR was its uniformity. All educational institutions - nursery to university, trade schools and also vocational schools for future artists (such as theater, music, dance, and art schools) were interlinked to form one system of education. The ultimate goal of the educational system of the GDR, stated in the form of an Act in 1965 and inserted into the GDR constitution in 1968, was to create "an educated socialist nation."[21] At first glance this may seem obvious, since the goal of any educational system should be to educate those who pass through it. However, the term "educated socialist nation" implied a nation, a whole nation, educated in the principles of socialism. This meant that a heavy component of socialist doctrine had to accompany any area of the educational system, whether in a nursery, a university, or an acting school. It was a requirement that all areas of instruction stress the inherent relationship between scientific, sociological processes and one's daily life. In fact, according to Marxist-Leninist theory, all areas of one's life, whether political, social, public, or private were tightly interrelated. Education, then, did not cease when one's school or university days were over, it pervaded all areas of life through literature, mass media, and especially theatre.

As far as theatre was concerned, all artists were to be subservient to the playwright, as it was through his or her hand that the message was formulated. Theatre was to be performed realistically, could not promote aesthetic abstraction, and was to focus on human consciousness and mankind's "world of things."[22] Preoccupation with art for its own sake, form, myth and mysticism of its any kind was not allowed. Art of this type promoted a shift of focus from the material world,

---

[20] Joachim Streisand, Kulturgeschichte der DDR: Studien su Ihren Historischen Grundlagen und Ihren Entwicklungsetappen (Köln: Pahl-Rugenstein Verlag, 1981), p. 98.

[21] Kurt Sontheimer The Government and Politics of East Germany (London: St.Martin's Press, 1975), p. 126.

allowed for non-productive distraction, and did not aid in the construction of socialism. Plays were judged on the basis of both content and form, and a play could be condemned for failing in either category. Plays simply had to be functional, supportive of the party, and accessible to the intellects and feelings of the majority of the people.

Stanislavski - The Model for Performance

When considering a model for realistic performance, East Germany looked to the Russian actor, director and theorist, Konstantin Stanislavski. The Stanislavski system had proven its compatibility with socialist doctrine several years earlier, as Stanislavski had warded off attacks against his system by those who attempted to label it as mystical and "dealing with psychology."[23] In order to satisfy the objectors, Stanislavski had explained several of the misunderstood facets of his program and changed the wording of several concepts. Eventually he achieved full support for his system by the highest Soviet officials, including Stalin.[24]

Prior to the formation of the GDR two of Stanislavski's texts had been available in German translation *Mein Leben in der Kunst*: (My Life in Art) and *Die Arbeit des Schauspielers an Sich Selbst* (The Work of the Actor on Himself)[25], both translated by the Swiss author Alexandra Meyenburg in 1939. The first extended study of Stanislavski's acting theories in Germany came in 1945, as Ottofritz Gaillard, Maxim Vallentin, and Otto Lang established a Stanislavski acting school at the *Staatliche Musikhochschule Weimar*. Gaillard, who had studied both acting and

---

[23] Alexander Afinogenov, Russian dramatist and philosopher led the attack, which took place at the conference of the Russian Association of Proletarian Writers in January 1931.

[24] H.G. Huettich, Theatre in the Planned Society: Contemporary Theatre in the German Democratic Republic (Chapel Hill: University of North Carolina Press, 1978), p. 14.

[25] known in the West as An Actor Prepares.

Theatrewissenschaft in Berlin[26] and Rostock, felt that the available translations of Stanislavski's theories were not helpful for actual theatre practice. Gaillard had been fortunate enough to receive practical training in the Stanislavski method with Ivan Schmith, a director at the *Deutsches Theater* and teacher at the *Schauspielschule des Deutschen Theaters*. Schmith had taught for only one year at the school, in 1934, but fortunately that year had coincided with Gaillard's first year of study at the *Schauspielschule*. Therefore, Gaillard's practical knowledge of the system served as the catalyst of the school at Weimar. Maxim Vallentin, the next of the founders, had escaped to the Soviet Union during Hitler's rise to power, returning to Germany in 1945 as part of a communist theatrical ensemble - the *Gruppe Ulbricht*. Vallentin championed the Soviet theatre, socialist realism, and the Stanislavski method, and upon his return published a brochure entitled "On the teachings of the Soviet Theater" (*Aus den Erfahrungen des Sowjettheaters*). Lang, a professor of drama at the *Staatliche Musikhochschule*, coordinated the effort, bringing Gaillard and Vallentin to join him in Weimar.

During the summer of 1947 the acting department at Weimar was enlarged to a complete drama school, and was renamed the *Deutsche Theaterinstitut*. The institute quickly became the German base for the teachings of Stanislavski, where both students and teachers could participate in the study of the Stanislavski method. That same year, Gaillard published *Das Deutsche Stanislavski Buch*, which became the accepted German interpretation of Stanislavski in the German Democratic Republic.[27] In the *Stanislavski Buch*, Gaillard summarized Stanislavski's method, providing his own examples related to the concepts. Overall, he offered a standard presentation of the concepts, focusing on physical action as the central concept. Chapter two includes a useful example of Gaillard's discussion. Utilizing the story of an amateur actor sitting nervously in a chair on stage, Gaillard notes how Stanislavski

---

[26]Gaillard studied at the *Schauspielschule des Deutschen Theaters* for one year, in 1934.
[27]Klaus Völker, Berlin, Germany, May 1993.

would stand beside him and search for something in his notebook. Soon, the student became aware of Stanislavski's presence and began to concentrate on him. This, Gaillard noted, gave the student a purpose, so the student would quit fidgeting and begin to concentrate on something specific. Gaillard later discusses the *als ob* or creative if, asking the actor to attempt to isolate situations that he/she had previously thought of or experienced. However, Gaillard takes a different approach to the "creative if" than the approach commonly discussed in the United States. Gaillard explains a scenario in which a student is asked to take hold of a hat, and hold it "as if" it were a dog. While this required the student to use his imagination, it had little to do with placing oneself within the life of the character, "as if you had experienced what the character had experienced up to that point in the character's life."[28] Since Stanislavski's theories were a recent phenomenon in 1947, minor inconsistencies could be expected. However, an examination of *Das Deutsche Stanislavski Buch* suggests no deliberate alterations in order to comply with political restrictions. The text appears to have been trusted as it was written.

Perhaps the essence of the approach adopted by Gaillard and his colleagues at the *Deutsche Theaterinstitut* was best presented in the preface to *Das Deutsche Stanislavski Buch*. Written by Maxim Vallentin, the preface acknowledged Hamlet's "advice to the player's" as the basis of realistic acting. Vallentin disclosed the three components of truth on the stage; "...first, the truth of acting discovery; second the societal truth; and finally the truth of the stage with the goal - to ground the truth in stage action."[29] Still in the preface, Vallentin later asks,

> Why Stanislavski? Isn't that something of a contemporary Russian model, suitable only for the theatre there? On the contrary: it is very old what he has taught; it is truth and nature. But it is the first and only, that of the

---

[28]Robert Barton, Acting: Onstage and Off (New York: Harcourt, Brace, Jovanovich Publishers, 1989), p. 106. Though this is an undergraduate acting text, it is felt that Barton represents the common view of Stanislvski by the American theatre community.

[29]Maxim Vallentin, quoted in Ottofritz Gaillard, *Das Deutsche Stanislavski Buch* (Berlin: Aufbau-Verlag, 1947), p. 10.

correct method of organic production. It is quite and simply - nature.[30]

The timing of the founders of the *Deutsche Theaterinstitut* was perfect. In 1948 several advocates of socialist realism in the GDR began "swinging a mallet vigorously" over writers and plays that they considered formalist.[31] Instigated by Fritz Erpenbeck, a dramaturg at the *Deutsches Theater* and one of the major writers of the East German publication Theater der Zeit, the charges were leveled against all non-socialist works. Erpenbeck stated that all plays which were not photographic casting of everyday reality should be considered formalist. Included among the works designated as formalist were those by Goethe, Schiller, and Shakespeare which were written in verse. The leaders of the *Deutsche Theaterinstitut* saw this as a golden opportunity to promote the work they were doing. Gaillard published an article in Theater der Zeit that stated:

> ... our work is based on the content of a play, from which we arrive at a central form; in non-socialist art the finished form in relation to the content has become mostly aesthetic. Should someone attempt to get along with these finished forms in theatre today, it would be impossible.[32]

Gaillard promoted the Stanislavski system as the center of an "artistic-communal education," in which the amount of artistic expression was responsibly measured.[33] Consequently, cultural officials began to condemn theatrical productions which did not employ photographic reproduction and the Stanislavski method. This struggle is best illustrated in the Commission's criticism of Brecht.

---

[30] Ibid., p. 11.

[31] Gerhard Ebert, Schauspieler Werden in Berlin (Berlin: Berlin-Information, 1987), p. 101.

[32] Ottofritz Gaillard, "*Neue Schauspielerziehung*," Theater der Zeit (December 1946), p. 36.

[33] Gerhard Ebert, Schauspieler Werden in Berlin (Berlin: Berlin-Information, 1987), p. 118.

Bertolt Brecht - The "Other" Approach

While Stanislavski was considered the basis of a socialist realistic form of theatre in the early years of the German Democratic Republic, the growing influence of Brecht would eventually force a compromise in the development of East German theatre aesthetics. Prior to his exile in Scandinavia and the United States (1933 - 1947), Brecht had laid the foundations for his theatrical style in Berlin. Upon his return to Berlin in 1948 Brecht returned to business as usual, but in time was faced with severe criticism from the East German social realists. Initially, Brecht's problems began with his now classic production of Mother Courage and Her Children at the *Deutsches Theater* on January 11, 1949. An attack was launched by the dramatist Frederich Wolf, who was concerned with the fact that Mother Courage did not change in the end, nor did she seem to gain a new social insight.[34] Brecht's reply is legendary:

> Dear Frederich Wolf, you, especially, will confirm that the playwright was a realist in that case. Even if Courage doesn't learn anything, the audience can, in my opinion, still learn something by watching her.[35]

Brecht's problems were just beginning. Three years later his view was labeled "objectivism" by the State Commission for Artistic Affairs. This came as the result of a running debate between Brecht and those who favored a more conservative approach to socialist realism. In a series of "Stanislavski" conferences organized by the Commission, there were attacks launched against both the style and substance of Brecht's productions. According to the Commission, there were three failing points to Brecht's previous works. Initially, his critical approach had presented negative observations of social reality; secondly, there had been no positive hero on stage; and

---

[34]H.G. Huettich, Theatre in the Planned Society: Contemporary Theatre in the German Democratic Republic (Chapel Hill: University of North Carolina Press, 1978(, p. 13.

[35]Bertolt Brecht, Brecht on Theatre trans. By John Willett (London: Methuen, 1964), p. 229.

finally, the image of a utopia had been presented in a clouded form.[36] Regarding Brecht's 1951 production of Gorki's The Mother, the Central Committee of the *SED* asked,

> Is this really realism? Are these typical characters in typical surroundings? [Not to] mention the form. This is not theatre; it is some kind of cross or synthesis of Meyerhold and the Cult of Proletarianism.[37]

The hardest blow came when Brecht's play The Last Days of the Commune (*Die Tage der Commune*) was denied production in 1952. The play, which dealt with the 1871 uprising of the Paris Commune in an objective, yet historically accurate manner, was labeled as "defeatist" and "objectivistic" by the Central Committee.[38] Brecht responded to the criticism by providing his own definition of socialist realism, which included:

> Socialist realism means realistically reproducing men's life together by artistic means from a socialist point of view. It is reproduced in such a way as to promote insight into society's mechanism's and stimulate socialist impulses...A socialist realist work of art shows characters and events as historical and alterable, and as contradictory. This entails a great change; a serious effort has to be made to find a new means of expression.[39]

Brecht's desire was that the theatre of East Germany would find its own means of expression, more effective than "propagandistic representations of contemporary social reality clothed in Stanislavski technique."[40] He felt that his style of production would be more effective for social change since the audience would be

---

[36] John Rouse, Brecht and the West German Theatre (Ann Arbor: University of Michigan Press, 1989), p. 58.

[37] H.G. Huettich, Theatre in the Planned Society: Contemporary Theatre in the German Democratic Republic (Chapel Hill: University of North Carolina Press, 1978.

[38] Ibid., p. 27.

[39] Bertolt Brecht, Brecht on Theatre trans. by John Willett (London: Methuen, 1964), p. 165.

[40] John Rouse, Brecht and the West German Theatre (Ann Arbor: University of Michigan Press, 1989), p. 59.

always aware that they were watching a play and not "tricked" into believing that what they were watching was real. His alienation effect would distance the spectators from the play, so they could view the action critically and witness it from a fresh point of view. Thus, Brecht argued that his theatre would be a more effective vehicle for social change.

Unfortunately, the changes Brecht proposed did not gain official acceptance until 1956, the year of his death. Through a series of articles published in Neue Deutsche Literatur, the East German dramatist Peter Hacks proposed a more dialectical view of realism based more evenly on the theories of Brecht and the Marxist philosopher Georg Lukacs. Hacks noted that the hero should possess "the typical contradictions of his society" and exist in "the typical contradictory situations of his period."[41] According to Hacks, a dramatist could chart one of two paths, by dramatizing the historical process in action, or by using poetic material to anticipate the course of history. Hacks noted that the drama of East Germany could become more formally sophisticated because society had embarked on a new quest for self-fulfillment. The direction suggested by Hacks and others later became known as the *Neue Sachlichkeit*, or new objectivity, and by 1957 the SED's official position towards drama allowed for new forms and experimentation. Thus two forms of drama became acceptable in the GDR: the more traditional socialist realism, and an experimental theater based on the theories of Brecht.[42]

All of these reforms in theatrical production were instrumental in the development of actor training institutions, because the methodology of the schools and the material performed in classrooms had to reflect the practice of the state theatres. It was in this political context that the *Staatliche Schauspielschule Berlin* was established.

---

[41] Marvin Carlson, Theories of the Theatre (Ithaca, N.Y.: Cornell University Press, 1984), p. 424.
[42] H.G. Huettich, Theatre in the Planned Society: Contemporary Theatre in the German Democratic Re

CHAPTER 4

STAATLICHE SCHAUSPIELSCHULE BERLIN

State Academies Established

In 1951, two years after the German Democratic Republic was formed, the State Commission for Artistic Affairs (*Staatlichen Kommission für Kunstangelegenheiten*) was established, with one of its first tasks being the reorganization of the training of young actors. The primary goal of the Commission was to ensure "that each gifted young person receive an education in the arts without concern for his/her financial situation."[1] The Commission believed that in the years prior to 1949 students from higher income levels had been able to devote all of their energy to study, while those from lower income brackets had been forced to take on part-time jobs in order to support themselves. Also, in the past the *Intendanten* of the theatres (in the case of Reinhardt, the director of the acting school) had exploited the young actors, forcing them into smaller roles and distracting them from their training program. The Commission felt that the type of mass education evidenced by previous efforts had produced a host of unqualified young actors who had learned their craft through performing supernumerary or secondary roles.[2] The commission proposed that the schools should be separated from theatres, that they should function as state or city schools, and that all students should be given stipends in order to fully focus

---

[1] Gerhard Ebert, Schauspieler Werden in Berlin (Berlin: Berlin-Information, 1987), p. 111.
[2] Ibid., p. 111.

on their training. Later that year (1951) three institutes for theatre training were established. The *Staatliche Schauspielschule Berlin* (hereafter referred to as the State Acting Academy of East Berlin) was established from the tradition of the *Schauspielschule des Deutsches Theater*. In Leipzig, the *Theaterhochschule "Hans Otto"* was established from the tradition of the *National Theaterinstitut Weimar*; and in Rostock, the *Staatliche Schauspielschule Rostock* was founded for professional theatre training in northern East Germany. Also established were three dance schools: the *Palucca-Schule* in Dresden, the *Fachschule für Tanz* in Leipzig, and the *Staatliche Balletschule* in Berlin; four schools for training in music: the *Deutsche Hochschule für Musik "Hans Eisler"* in Berlin, the *Hochschule für Musik "Felix Mendelssohn-Bartholdy"* in Leipzig, the *Franz-Liszt-Hochschule* in Weimar, and the *Hochschule für Musik "Carl Maria Von Weber"* in Dresden; two schools of art and design: the *Künsthochschule Berlin* and the *Hochschule für bildende Künst in Dresden*; and one film school, the *Hochschule für Film und Fernsehen "Konrad Wolf"*. All of the institutes for artistic training were under the auspices of the Ministry of Culture of the GDR, in consultation with the Academy of Arts, the Association of Theatricians of the GDR, and the Artist's Trade Union.[3] In addition to artistic training in theatre, it was possible to study theatre arts as an academic discipline in the GDR. Degrees in theatre were offered at *Humbolt Universität* and at *Universität Leipzig*. Professional degrees as voice pedagogues for the stage were offered at both the *Universität Halle* and *Humbolt Universität*.

With the beginning of state-sanctioned artistic training in the GDR the Ministry of Culture guaranteed three things to prospective students of the arts: that there would be an equitable number of training schools (13) in relation to the population; that students would be guaranteed stipends during their matriculation;

---

[3] Center GDR of the International Theatre Institute, <u>Theatre in the German Democratic Republic</u>, Vol.6 (Berlin: Center GDR of the International Theatre Institute, 1972), p. 4.

and, that upon graduation, students would be guaranteed jobs in East German State theaters by the Central Theatre Agency.[4]

Staatliche Schauspielschule Berlin

The State Acting Academy of East Berlin was chartered in 1951 as one of the four centers for the training of actors.[5] The academy was formed by the merger of the *Schauspielschule of the Deutsches Theater* (formerly the Reinhardt school) with the Acting Class of the United German Film Studios (*Deutsche Film-Aktiengesellschaft* or *DEFA*). Professors, materials, and financial reserves from both institutions were joined together to create the initial structure of the academy, with state subsidy providing supplemental funds. After the first year, the academy was a unified, state-funded entity.

With the separation of Germany in 1949, Wolfgang Langhoff, for many years the administrative "caretaker" of the academy, realized that a more dynamic leader, committed to the changes taking place in the newly formed German Democratic Republic, was needed. Langhoff summoned Otto Dierichs, who had worked with him at the *Deutsches Theater*, and offered him the position. Dierichs, then in Dresden, accepted the position on the condition that he be allowed to make changes as necessary. Initially, Dierichs felt that the Academy needed a permanent home with improved facilities. In consultation with Langhoff, Dierichs chose to move the academy to an old boathouse in Schöneweide, approximately ten miles south of downtown Berlin. Dierichs was motivated to move the school to Schöneweide in order to remove the students from the distractions of downtown Berlin and to place them beyond the reach of all the theatres that wanted to use them as supernumeraries

---

[4]Ibid., p. 3.

[5]*The Hochschule für Film und Fernsehen "Konrad Wolf"* had a division for training actors, therefore it is normally considered a fourth acting school.

in their productions. Dierichs felt that the most negative aspect of the Reinhardt system had been assigning the students small roles in the productions at the *Deutsches Theater*, thereby decreasing the time they could spend in studio work. He felt that one did not learn to act by playing small roles, and that the practice had been a matter of convenience for the theatre but a disservice to the students.[6] Furthermore, in keeping with the spirit of the newly formed German Democratic Republic, Dierichs hoped to create a bond with the large base of working class citizens located in Schöneweide. This was accomplished by providing small touring productions to various workplaces in Schöneweide and by offering local people special studio productions at the Academy.[7]

Dierichs received his theatre education at the *Louise Dumont Schule* in Dusseldorf, acted and directed professionally for several years in Dresden, and worked from 1939 until 1945 as a university professor in the actor training program at the *Hochschule für Theater Essen*. "Under my leadership" he stated, "we will completely revise the essence of (theater) education in the DDR."[8] He felt that the greatest problem, in addition to the attachment of schools to resident theater companies, was the fact that most classes were taught by the leading actors and directors of the theaters. Teaching was of secondary importance for them as their artistic work was their primary concern. Dierichs noted that the fact that they were performers did not necessarily qualify them as proficient teachers. He complained that there was a "lack of good instructors" at the organized acting schools, and that many of the best teachers taught privately. On the other hand, Dierichs pointed out that even the best private teachers could not instruct in all necessary areas. Through additional funding and other incentives he attracted to the state theatre schools better-qualified teachers for whom teaching was of primary interest.

---

[6]Gerhard Ebert, Schauspieler Werden in Berlin (Berlin: Berlin-Information, 1987), p. 113.
[7]Ibid., p. 113.
[8]Ibid., p. 112.

Dierichs noted that the chief characteristic of Reinhardt's school at the *Deutsches Theater* had been an "eclectic approach," based on the teachings of Reinhardt. However, while Reinhardt had maintained an interest in pluralistic training and a multiplicity of viewpoints, Dierichs felt that he (Reinhardt) had prepared actors for only one theatre, the *Deutsches Theater*. He wanted to develop a "school for all theaters," in which an actor would be able to perform for a number of different theaters after graduation.[9] This could only be accomplished, Dierichs felt, with the implementation of a standardized methodology. An actor could not be expected to learn one particular style for Reinhardt, one for Vallentin, one for Brecht, and so on.

However, because of the criticism of the Brechtian approach that grew out of the Stanislavski conferences, the issue was not satisfactorily resolved until the work of Rudolf Penka in the 1960s. Until then, students were taught primarily through the basis of models and model performances.[10] To supplement their Stanislavski based exercises, students were coached to copy the great performances of actors such as Ernst Busch, Helene Weigel, and Willy A. Kleinau. Theatre students were able to watch the great performers on GDR stages, work with professors who had directed them, and read written documentation of model performances, such as Brecht's 1949 Mother Courage at the *Deutsches Theater*.

This was a transition time for the academy not only in terms of locale, but also in terms of staffing and approach. One of the chief reasons was simply a matter of discontinuity, since none of the original teachers from the Reinhardt era were there any more. Dierichs had no attachment to Reinhardt or to Reinhardt's system, because he had not studied at the *Schauspielschule des Deutschen Theaters*. Most of the others who had worked with or studied under Reinhardt had either retired or died. Gertrud Eyesoldt, perhaps the greatest acting teacher under Reinhardt, had died in

---

[9]Friedrich Anders, "*Schauspieler Brauchen Wir*" Theater der Zeit (October 1951): 4-5.

[10]Hans-Georg Voigt "*Arbeit an einer Szene UnterBenutzung eines Modells*" Stockholmer Protokoll: Aus der Arbeit der Staatliche Schauspielschule Berlin (Berlin: Henschel Verlag, 1969), p. 37.

1950. Eduard von Winterstein, who had been an acting teacher at the school since its beginning, retired at 80 years old. Much of the tradition and instructional methodology of the school had been corrupted during the Nazi years and almost completely lost during World War II.[11]

In September 1951 the new State acting academies became were officially established.[12] Dierichs, chair of the school curriculum committee of State Commission for Artistic Affairs drafted several articles of reorganization. The curriculum of the new State Acting Academy of East Berlin was modeled on the established precepts of both the *Schauspielschule des Deutschen Theaters* and the *Deutsche TheaterInstitut Weimar*.[13] The Stanislavski method, as prescribed by Gaillard, was viewed as the recommended approach to acting along with work on model performances. Regarding the practice of students working as supernumeraries while in school, a policy was established that students could accept no professional work, including small parts with the local professional theatres, during their first two years of study. After that, it was decided students should occasionally be allowed to work in professional theatres as long as it did not interfere with their studies. In 1953 the school curriculum committee of the State Commission for Artistic Affairs released the following statement:The objective of the education for the acting schools is training for the social realist theatre. That means foremost the training of the Stanislavski method and the mastery of physical actions.[14]

Dierichs remained as director of the school until 1956. After Dierichs, Lore Espey was appointed to a one-year term as director, but was quickly replaced as it was felt that she had "wrong impressions of Stanislavski's system."[15] Once again

---

[11]Ibid., p. 118.

[13]Acting instructors were sent to Weimar during the summer of 1952 for an intensive Stanislavski seminar, under the direction of Maxim Vallentin and Ottofritz Gaillard.

[14]Gerhard Ebert, Schauspieler Werden in Berlin (Berlin: Berlin-Information, 1987), p. 121.

[15]Ibid., p. 127.

Langhoff stepped in to provide guidance for several years while the leadership of the school was divided among several professors.

Program of Study at the State Acting Academy

The State Acting Academy of East Berlin was instituted as a three year vocational program in acting, and remained that way until 1984 when a fourth year of study was added.[16] No additional coursework was included in the fourth year; instead, the students engaged in a series of studio productions. The three year program at the academy consisted of study in three areas: 1) the practical areas of acting, voice and speech, diction, music, dance, acrobatics, stage fencing, and make-up; 2) academic areas of theatre such as theatre history, dramatic theory, and aesthetics; 3) and finally, in keeping with the policies of the socialist education system of the GDR, students were instructed in the areas of Marxist-Leninist theory, political economy, the history of the workers' movement, theories of society, and Russian language. The primary goal of the academy was to prepare actors and actresses for work in the state supported theatres of the German Democratic Republic. This required the curriculum to maintain a significant amount of practical and ideological coursework designed to simultaneously promote the student's talent, knowledge, and social awareness, so that they would become socially conscious actors. Education at the academy consisted of artistic training within the larger context of society, so that the students would develop their acting approach in harmony with a scientific world education and a sense of artistic responsibility.[17] Acting classes were conducted in two basic formats: improvisation and scene study (*szenestudium*). Improvisation classes were held during the first two semesters of the student's matriculation, in

---

[16] The *Staatliche Schauspielschule* was granted *Hochschule* status in 1981 and the name was changed to the *Hochschule für Schauspielkunst "Ernst Busch."*

[17] Gerhard Piens "*Die Staatliche Schauspielschule Berlin*" Stockholmer Protokoll: Aus der Arbeit der Staatliche Schauspielschule Berlin (Berlin: Henschel Verlag, 1969), p. 10.

larger groups of between fifteen and twenty students. During the initial weeks of the first semester, students were asked to improvise concrete situations that they had actually observed; simple excerpts from their daily lives recreated exactly as they occurred. In order to ground their action in the physical world, the use of material possessions was also suggested. Throughout the improvisation seminar students explored the dialectic of improvisation and fixation, believing that the creative process invented during improvisation can only be captured when the actor has learned to repeat events unmechanically and therefore creatively. The process, still in use at the *HfSK*, is explored at greater length in chapter six.

Scene study sessions, beginning in the second year of a student's training, lasted for approximately six weeks. Included in each group were one teacher or director and four to six students, with each being assigned a substantial scene from a particular play. Contemporary dramatic literature was favored during the student's second year, with classical drama becoming the focus of the third year. Each group spent about four hours for three days each week rehearsing the scene. Because of the small group and the number of hours of rehearsal, each group was able to delve into the specific details of the scene for extended periods of time. At the end of the session, the results of the work were presented to an invited group of teachers and students from the Academy, who subsequently critiqued the scene. This format replaced the previous format of actor training in Germany, consisting of a master teacher and his assistants who taught a group of ten to twelve students for three or four years and imparted his method to them.

More important than the structures of individual classes were the concepts employed by the Academy. Because of the influence of both Brecht and Stanislavski on theatre in the German Democratic Republic, the goal of acting instruction was to link the two concepts together.[18] This theoretical position was

---

[18] Rudolf Penka, "*Arbeitserfahrungen mit Stanislavski und Brecht*," in Schauspielen Handbuch, ed. Gerhard Ebert and Rudolf Penka (Berlin: Henschel Verlag, 1988), p. 35.

advanced by a man who is considered one of the greatest acting teachers in the long history of the Reinhardt *Schauspielschule*/State Acting Academy/Ernst Busch School: Rudolf Penka.

Leadership of the Staatliche Schauspielschule Berlin (1962 - 1989)

Any discussion concerning the history and methodology of the *Staatliche Schauspielschule Berlin* must acknowledge the influence of Penka. So much of the actor training process, the theory behind the process, and so many of the successful actors who graduated from the *Schauspielschule*, were the product of Rudi Penka. Penka was born on March 29, 1923 in Moravska, Czechoslovakia. Penka's father, a member of the Czech working class, was co-founder of the Communist party in Czechoslovakia. Following in his father's footsteps, Penka was a member of several political groups - the Communist Youth Association of Czechoslovakia and a highly vocal anti-fascist group formed in 1942 after the Nazi occupation of Czechoslovakia. Arrested in 1943 and later imprisoned for insubordination, he was freed by Soviet troops in May, 1945, and moved to Germany in 1946.[19]

In 1947 Penka enrolled at the University of Leipzig where he studied German, philosophy, and history. He was a member of the student acting group, and eventually decided to move his career in the direction of theatre. He went on to study at the *Theaterhochschule "Hans Otto"* in Leipzig, later working as an instructor from 1955 until 1959. During his stay in Leipzig he acted professionally at the *Theater der Jungen Welt* and spent one season at the *Deutsches Nationaltheater* in Weimar as both actor and director. However, it was his talent for teaching and interest in acting theory that would make Penka one of the most respected acting teachers in East Germany. In 1960 he was appointed as leader of the acting division at the State Acting Academy of East Berlin, and in 1962 he was appointed Director of the

---

[19] Gerhardt Ebert, Schauspieler Werden in Berlin (Berlin: Berlin-Information, 1987), p. 154.

Academy. Between 1962 and 1964 Penka made several trips to Russia and sat in on acting classes at two of the Soviet Union's best theatre schools - the Moscow State Institute of Theatre, the largest of Moscow's schools, and the Leningrad Institute of Theatre, Music and Cinematography. He analyzed the curriculum and structural philosophy of the two institutes, comparing the programs in Russia with that of the State Acting Academy of East Berlin in order to make alterations or changes if appropriate. Penka was especially impressed with the standardized format of each year of study at the schools of the Soviet Union: first year - improvisational training and basic exercises; second year - beginning scene work; third year - longer scenes (a whole act); fourth year - a whole play. Penka brought many principles back to Berlin and implemented them at the Academy. In 1966, two years after his return from the Soviet Union, Penka was awarded the title of Professor.[20]

Perhaps Penka's greatest accomplishment at the State Acting Academy came in 1967 in Stockholm, Sweden, at the Acting Symposium of the International Theatre Institute. The theme of the symposium was "Vocational Training for the Actor," and covered such areas as social and cultural aspects of training, and the differing styles of acting which are required by different texts. Five schools were invited to Stockholm by the International Theatre Institute: the Central School for Speech and Drama, London; the *Hochschule für Schauspielkunst*, Strasbourg; the *Staatliche Schauspielschule Berlin*; the *Univerzitet Umetnosti U Beogradu* (Academy for Theatre, Film, Television, and Radio Belgrad), and the *Kunigliche Teaterhogsköle Stockholm* (State School for Theater Training, Stockholm). Prior to the schools' arrival in Stockholm each of the five schools had been asked to prepare two scenes, to be presented as part of the symposium. An advisory committee assigned two playwrights to each of the schools, from whose repertoire of dramatic work they were to present one scene each (a total of two scenes per school). The Strasbourg School was assigned Moliere and Brecht; the Stockholm school was assigned Strindberg and

---

[20]Ibid. p. 156.

Pinter; the Belgrad school was assigned Chekhov and Strindberg; the Central School of London was assigned Pinter and Moliere, and the Berlin School was assigned Chekhov and Brecht.[21] The schools could make their own choice as to which play and scenes that they would present. The committee also requested that each school demonstrate acting/movement exercises, discuss acting methodology, and comment on the process of the development of these scenes for a period of fifteen minutes after the scenes were presented.

The State Acting Academy chose to present a scene from Brecht's Mr. Puntilla and His Man Matti (*Herr Puntilla und Sein Mann Matti*), directed by Hans-Georg Voigt, and a scene from Chekhov's The Wedding Proposal (*Heiratsantrag*), directed by Rudolf Penka. Dr. Gerhard Piens, an instructor from the academy, was chosen to deliver the speech regarding the school's methodology.

At the end of the competition, the State Acting Academy of East Berlin placed first. The committee of judges, led by Michel St. Denis of France, cited the "clarity of objective and success of their method...a cleverness, certainty and simplicity with which the students presented their work." as the reason for the success of the Berlin school.[22] Walter Felsenstein, President of the Center DDR of the International Theatre Institute, who was present at the competition stated:

> At the schools which are concerned with theatre, I am convinced that it is rare to find a well-conceived methodology and thorough education. The best that I know is the *Staatliche Schauspielschule Berlin* under the direction of Rudi Penka.[23]

Work With Brecht and Stanislavski

Throughout Penka's tenure at the academy (1962-1975), he was

---

[21] This documentation was found in the introduction to Stockholmer Protokoll: Aus der Arbeit der Staatliche Schauspielschule Berlin (Berlin: Henschel Verlag, 1969), p. 4.

[22] Ibid., p. 6.

[23] Gerhard Ebert, Schauspieler Werden in Berlin (Berlin: Berlin-Information, 1987), p. 180.

continually faced with what had become a large issue in the German Democratic Republic: how to link together the acting methodologies of Stanislavski and Brecht. Previously, the two methodologies had been considered polemic opposites; irreconcilable performance approaches.[24] However, given the fact that plays based in both approaches made up the bulk of the repertoire in the German Democratic Republic, it became apparent that some reconciliation was necessary. Penka confronted the issue by stating that it was too confusing to attempt to train actors to act one way for Brecht plays, and another way for the realistic "Stanislavski-dominated" theatre. He pointed out that stylistic concerns were less important than focus on the task of producing believable characters. He felt that research into both theories would yield some common ground, which would then serve as the basis for a compatible acting technique. Once accomplished, Penka hoped to arrive, at least in theory, at an acting methodology that would yield a truthfulness of both form and content.

Penka's inquiry consisted of both lectures and practical work in acting classes at the State Acting Academy, with documentation of the sessions published in a series of articles written between 1965 and 1975. While there is little information describing the actual practice, much of the thought behind the process is useful. The basis of Penka's analysis was the isolation of a set of characteristics common to both approaches. Initially, Penka examined what he regarded as misconceptions about the work of each. According to Penka, Stanislavski's "truth of feeling" had often resulted in acting that was individualistic and anarchistic. Wrongly interpreted, the search for truth of feeling led to self-centered and self-indulgent acting. Also, Penka felt that the type of truth that had been sought for at the *Deutsche Theaterinstitut Weimar* had been limiting to actors, because students were limited to playing characters with which their age and realm of experience coincided. This severely limited the

---

[24]John Rouse, Brecht and the West German Theatre Ann Arbor: University of Michigan Press, 1989) p. 57.

development of the students' sense of fantasy and creation. Brecht's theory of alienation had also been misunderstood, according to Penka, which in production resulted in formalistic body attitudes and emotionless behavior.[25] Both Stanislavski and Brecht, he noted, had become associated with a mode or fashion, thereby clouding the essence of their work. Therefore, the first step of Penka's inquiry consisted of defining the essential qualities of each. He saw the influence of modernism in Stanislavski, who exposed the "essential in art," presenting the humanistic substance of character. Central to the Stanislavski technique was the idea of "ethic," the discipline involved in the creation of a living art form. However Stanislavski's work was not limited to work on the individual. Penka pointed out that Stanislavski's method was developed "in the collective life of the theatre ensemble, where there were no stars, just performers who made up a family of theatre artists."[26] Brecht, on the other hand, presented an art form characterized by it's "withdrawal from the endeavor," focusing on aesthetic attractions of the character. Yet like Stanislavski's method, Brecht's was an "art of observation." Both approaches required the actor "to see and watch, to hear and listen - but they must happen in that order!"[27] The actor was to become an active observer and co-creator of the societal environment on stage. Stanislavski and Brecht were seeking to present truth on stage, therefore truth was isolated as another common element of the two theories.[28] However, the truth both were seeking was not the truth of the past, but the truth of the present. He pointed out that for Brecht truth meant "the production of new artistic means, with the destruction of old ones."[29] Next, Penka noted that both

---

[25] Rudolf Penka, "*Arbeitserfahrungen mit Stanislavski und Brecht*" Schauspielen Handbuch ed. Gerhard Ebert and Rudolf Penka (Berlin: Henschel Verlag, 1988), p. 35.

[26] Ibid., p. 36.

[27] Ibid., p. 36.

[28] This does seem simplistic, but nevertheless this was his starting point in the published work "*Arbeitserfahrung mit Stanislavski und Brecht.*"

[29] Ibid., p. 38.

Stanislavski and Brecht asked that the actor think on stage, and at times "not to know" the outcome of on stage events. But the most important principle was:

> ...the adoption of universally accepted human behavior under specific scenic conditions, by which the usual atmosphere of an auditorium or room is transformed into a special place, with scenic elements, lighting, and a place for spectators.[30]

Penka continually stated that there was no "recipe" for training actors. Referring to Stanislavski's <u>Work of the Actor on Himself</u> Penka explained;

> There is no 'system.' There is only nature. The laws of art are not different from those of nature. . . a child is born and grows like a tree; a character must be approached in the same way.[31]

He believed that painfully exacting work in performing basic tasks on stage was the basis of all acting. The actor's problem rested in the fact that he had to arrive at an "organic authenticity" rather than superficiality in the execution of these tasks. Penka felt that the greatest ammunition for actors was the accumulation of "treasured experiences" along with a basic knowledge of social sciences. This gave the actor the necessary experiential knowledge, fundamental to Stanislavski, and insight into social relations for Brecht's social *gestus*.

<u>Hans-Peter Minetti</u>

Because of failing health, Rudolf Penka was forced to step down as director of the Academy in the spring of 1975. On April 9th of that year Hans-Peter Minetti, a professor at the State Acting Academy and prominent actor in the German Democratic Republic, was appointed director. This would mark yet another shift in

---

[30] Ibid., p. 40.
[31] Ibid., p. 36.

the direction of the academy, as Minetti placed greater emphasis on the use of actors in a socialist society.[32]

Minetti, son of the actor Bernard Minetti, was born in Berlin on April 21, 1926. He studied History and Philosophy at the Universities of Kiel, Hamburg, and at Berlin's *Humbolt Universität*. In 1945 he joined the *KPD* (Communist Party of Germany) and remained an active member throughout his career. Minetti studied with Maxim Vallentin and Ottofritz Gaillard at the *Deutsches Nationaltheater Weimar*, touring with the young ensemble in 1950. Later he had lengthy engagements with the *Staatliche Theater Schwerin, Maxim Gorki Theater*, and finally the *Deutsches Theater*, with guest appearances at the *Theater am Palast* and the *Volksbühne*. He starred in several major German films and also had a successful television career. Minetti's primary legacy was instilling into the actors a solid set of socialist beliefs. According to Minetti, actors needed "more than talent," to be a successful actor in the GDR. They had to have "unshatterable beliefs on the side of the workers," and not only be aware of the truth, but knowledgeable of the "why" of society, with a thorough grounding in socialist ideology. Minetti wrote,"the education of actors, is not separate from the society in which they exist, nor are the theatres for which they are contracted."[33]

During his tenure, from 1975 to 1981, "political" literary programs and also political musicals became signature events for the academy. These programs were open to the public on occasion, and other times toured throughout Schöneweide. Though Minetti's leadership was viewed as positive by the East German authorities, he was later criticized for overstressing the theoretical side of the actor's education.[34]

The late 1970s and the first half of the 1980s marked one of the most

---

[32] Gerhard Ebert, Schauspieler Werden in Berlin (Berlin: Berlin-Information, 1987), p. 193.
[33] Ibid., p. 193.
[34] Klaus Völker, Berlin, Germany, May 1993.

prolific periods of the State Acting Academy of East Berlin. As the GDR was experiencing greater political stability and growth in the world market, greater emphasis was placed on culture and artistic production. The number of professional theatre companies had grown to just over 100, with approximately two hundred performances taking place on a daily basis.[35] This was remarkable, considering the GDR was a country approximately the size of Ohio with just over seventeen million inhabitants. Theatre attendance was also very high during this period, for three basic reasons: low cost tickets (one to fifteen *marks*); organized group attendance and subscriptions, and very high artistic quality.[36] The academy had been able to attract the very best teachers available in the GDR, thereby making it the most desirable for students. Along with Penka, Minetti, and Gaillard - who had come to the academy in 1969 - were Friedo Solter, one of the most respected directors in the history of the *Deutsches Theater*, and Thomas Langhoff, son of Wolfgang Langhoff and as of 1994, *Intendant* of the *Deutsches Theater*. On average twelve hundred students made application to the program yearly, with twenty accepted.[37]

With the growing reputation of the State Acting Academy of East Berlin greater expectations were placed on the school and the type of graduates it produced. Pressure came from the managers of the state theatres to employ more practice and less theory in the education. 1978 Karl Schneider, *Intendant* of the *Staatstheater Magdeburg*, complained of the ineffectiveness of the school's methodology. Schneider stated that it was impossible to train a performer who was skilled in every method without confusing them.[38] Schneider felt strongly that the theatre companies themselves should provide training and education in socialist ideals and that if there were schools, only basic technique should be offered. Schneider's outcry had an

---

[35] Herbert Lederer, Handbook of East German Drama 1945-1985 (New York: Peter Lang, 1991), p. 1.
[36] Ibid., p. 2.
[37] Gerhard Ebert, Schauspieler Werden in Berlin (Berlin: Berlin-Information, 1987), p. 202.
[38] Ibid., p. 204.

opposite effect however, as it mobilized the faculty of the State Acting Academy to seek status as a "National School of Theatre." After petitioning the Commission for Artistic Affairs and undergoing a thorough review of its educational program, the Academy was granted the status of *Hochschule*. This afforded the State Acting Academy a larger budget, more faculty members, and the ability to award, for the first time, a *Diplom*, an academic certificate certifying completion of a state-approved course of study. In its recommendations the Commission approved construction of a new structure, additional faculty members, and the addition of a program in directing.

CHAPTER 5

THE HOCHSCHULE FÜR SCHAUSPIELKUNST "ERNST BUSCH."

This chapter is divided into two sections. Part one will continue the historical overview of the school from 1981 until the present, including information regarding the unification process and how that affected the *HfSK*. Part two will provide a description and an analysis of the facilities, philosophy, and curriculum of the *HfSK*. The information presented in Part II of this chapter was gathered by the author during two visits to the *HfSK*, the first during May of 1992, and the second during May and June of 1993.

Part I - Hochschule Status and the Eighties

Ernst Busch

With the beginning of the 1981/82 semester the State Acting Academy of East Berlin was renamed the *Hochschule für Schauspielkunst 'Ernst Busch' Berlin*. This also marked the first semester in a new building, situated next to the existing structure, which had also undergone extensive renovation. The new building and status were confirmed and commemorated on September 21, 1981 in a ceremony, attended by dozens of German actors, theatre personnel, school officials, and political leaders.[1] During this ceremony the school was officially granted the power to issue

---

[1] Gerhard Ebert, Schauspieler Werden in Berlin (Berlin: Berlin-Information, 1987), p. 220

a *Diplom* to its graduates, and Hans-Peter Minetti, the director of the academy, was endowed with the title of Rektor.

The name of the great German actor Ernst Busch was chosen to accompany the school's new title. Ernst Busch is best remembered as one of Brecht's favorite actors, and as a figurehead of the Communist Party of Germany. The *HfSK* was named after him because of his commitment to Communist ideals, his unusual level of self-discipline and work habits, and his great acting talent. Busch studied privately under Brecht, and during the 1950's and 60's played leading roles at the *Berliner Ensemble*, including the title role in Galileo, Azdak in The Caucasian Chalk Circle, and Pawel in Die Mutter. Busch had a very prolific film career, starring in one of the most famous German "working class" films, Kuhle Wampe. However, he is perhaps best remembered for his singing, performing ballads at the rallies of the Communist Party (*KPD*) in Berlin. Busch released over a dozen albums during the 1960's, singing with his memorable scratchy, and slightly off-pitch voice. While delivering the commemoration speech at the dedication ceremony of the *HfSK*, Hans-Joachim Hoffman, the Chief Minister of Culture of the GDR in 1981, said of Busch:

> Ernst Busch was raised by a working class family of the German proletariat class...He learned very early the problems and struggle of the workers. Busch had a deep love for men, the people, and for his class, which influenced him to join the communist arty very early in his life. His deep commitment to his ideals allowed him to assume a towering position on the German stage.[2]

Many changes accompanied the conversion of the State Acting Academy to the *HfSK*. A better facility for full-length productions was included in the new structure and was named the *Studiobühne "Wolfgang Heinz."* The *Institute für Schauspielregie* (Institute for Directing), which had been associated with the State Acting Academy since 1974, was officially annexed as part of the *HfSK*. The

---

[2]Ibid., p. 222.

Institute, located in Prenzlauer Berg just north of downtown East Berlin, produced a full season of productions and operated much like any of Berlin's other resident theatres with its full company and rotating repertory of plays. The new "Ernst Busch" school had a large "in-house" studio theatre on the main campus in addition to a fully equipped theatre and directing institute. At that point it was possible to implement a goal that the school had long hoped to realize: a fourth year of study in which the actors could spend the entire year practicing their craft. By 1984 the school had a four-year program in acting, directing, and in puppet-theatre.

Hochschule status afforded the "Ernst Busch" school a larger budget[3] and the ability to hire more of the best professors and guest instructors. During this time the school reclaimed its previous close working relationship with practically all of the major theatres in East Berlin, employing actors, directors, and voice and movement coaches from the theatres as instructors. This relationship afforded the students at the *HfSK* the distinct advantage of foregoing "internships" in the provinces and allowed them to obtain their initial contracts with major theatres in Berlin, the theatre capital of East Germany.

In 1987 Professor Kurt Veth, succeeded Hans-Peter Minetti as Rektor. Veth had worked with Brecht at the Berliner Ensemble from 1949-1954, and later directed plays in practically all the major theatres in Berlin and Dresden. His association with the school dates back until the late fifties, as he was an acting scene study teacher at the *Staatliche Schauspielschule Berlin*. He brought to the school the Brechtian philosophy that,

> the young actor should learn to narrate and not to impersonate. They should learn, one from the other, and not one or the other to play. They should learn, to make the spectator watch the group of actions and not to be anxious for the end, to convey knowledge to the spectator and not experience, to address his activity and not his emotions.[4]

---

[3] Exact budget figures for these years were not made available to me. However, I was informed by Professor Veth that the 1992 budget was in the 10.6 million mark range.

[4] Kurt Veth, Berlin, Germany, May 1992.

With his strong connections to the Berlin professional theatre, Veth was able to continue to place graduates of the *HfSK* at not only the best theatres in Germany, but in the best theatres in Berlin. He stated in 1992, "I do not wish to brag, but I can safely say that between 1981 and today, we have trained practically all of the great actors in the Berlin theatre."[5]

Among those teaching at the *HfSK* during this period were the established professors - Ottofritz Gaillard and Rudolf Penka, formulators of the acting methodology at the school; Friedo Solter and Thomas Langhoff, graduates of the school who were working at the Deutsches Theater and had returned to teach on a part-time basis; Hildegaard Buchwald-Wegeleben, a graduate of the Reinhardt school who had been the primary movement instructor since 1946; and Peter Kleinert and Peter Schroth, founders of the *Regieinstitut*. Newer professors and guest instructors included Gertrud Elisabeth Zillmer, engaged with the *Berliner Ensemble* since 1945; Ulrich Engelmann, an actor/director with the *Maxim Gorki Theater* since 1975; Hans-Georg Simmgen, from 1958-1968 engaged at the *Berliner Ensemble*; and Hans-Dieter Meves, from 1964 a director at the *Deutsches Theater*.

The actor-training program had acquired a slight sense of eclecticism, due to the influx of new viewpoints. Stanislavski was still the main influence, followed by Brecht, with most professors achieving a comfortable mix of the two. Following the success at the Stockholm Symposium in 1969, the division of acting had adopted the term "Penka Method" to describe their approach.[6] Rudolf Penka remained at the *HfSK*, teaching the Improvisation Seminar until his death in 1990.

German Reunification

In 1989, after several years of internal crisis, the German Democratic

---

[5]Ibid.

[6]Gerhard Ebert, Schauspieler Werden in Berlin (Berlin: Berlin-Information, 1987), p. 229.

Republic began to dissolve. The "construction of Socialism," a term utilized by party officials to describe the multifarious changes in the GDR, had created a powerful police state. The deep sense of repression coupled with random police brutality resulted in a series of demonstrations, many eventually resulting in riots. Finally, in November of 1989 the Berlin Wall was torn open, signaling free transport from East to West. Although a complete account of the disintegration of East Germany lies outside the scope of this study, it is important to include several facts which describe the reaction of the theatre community to the changes with began to occur in the GDR, beginning in the mid-seventies.

One of the first reactionary movements occurred after the expulsion of Wolf Bierman. Bierman's revolutionary ballads questioned the direction of East German socialism, resulting in his being labeled "arrogant and cynical" by *SED* Secretary General Erich Honecker.[7] In 1976 Bierman was stripped of his East German citizenship and expelled. In protest of this and other actions several artists and intellectuals began to flee East Germany, many relocating to West Germany and publicly voicing their displeasure with the GDR. In East German theatres a socially critical drama had emerged, including Ulrich Plenzdorf's *Die neuen Leiden des jungen W* (The New Sorrows of Young W.) in 1972, and Hermann Kant's *Das Impressum* (The Imprint) in 1976. Both works presented a hybrid form of socialist realism, with the positive hero at odds with his society instead of in harmony with it.[8]

The early eighties were characterized by a growing tension between the East and West, which reached a near climax with the Soviet invasion of Afghanistan in 1979-80. Living in uncertain political and economic conditions, many GDR citizens attempted to leave, forcing the *Stasi* (*Staatsicherheit* or Ministry for State Security) to take a more aggressive stance. *Stasi* activities escalated throughout the

---

[7]H.G. Huettich, Theatre in the Planned Society: Contemporary Drama in the German Democratic Republic (Chapel Hill: University of North Carolina Press, 1978), p. 134.
[8]Ibid., p. 151.

eighties, ranging from telephone tapping, to interrogation, to physical assault.[9] As early as April of 1989 East German theater artists engaged in a series of demonstrations, protesting random acts of violence against citizens. The first took place in Alexanderplatz, one of the most accessible gathering areas in East Berlin. Other protests were staged by theatre personnel in Halle, Mecklenberg, Dresden and Rostock. At the culmination of each demonstration, a list of grievances against the state was outlined; for example, the list compiled by the ensemble of the Dresden State Theater stated, 1) We have the right to information; 2) We have the right to open dialogue; 3) We have the right to individual thought and creativity; 4) We have the right to pluralistic thought; 5) We have the right to contradict; 6) We have the right to free travel; 7) We have the right to investigate our state leadership.[10] After being compiled and signed by those involved in the protests, the lists were sent to the Ministry of Culture of the GDR, printed in several underground newspapers, and prominently posted in public areas (such as Alexanderplatz). The series of demonstrations organized by East German theatre artists culminated on October 15th at the *Deutsches Theater* as another public forum was held, demanding investigation into the activities of the *Stasi* and Police (*Polizei*). These activities, organized by the East German theatrical community, though not the only organized demonstrations against the state during 1989, were among the most visible. They helped to set in motion the final series of events which led to the dismantling of the Berlin Wall in November 1989.[11]

With the reunification of Germany came the unification of all aspects of society, including cultural and educational institutions. The *HfSK* was incorporated

---

[9] Robert Darnton, "Stasi Besieged," in The Reunification of Germany, edited by Robert Emmett Long (New York: H.W. Wilson, 1992), p 61.

[10] Lennartz, Kurt. Theater in der DDR: Vom Aufbruch zur Wende. Sonderdruck: Erhard Friedrich Verlag, 1992. p. 58.

[11] These events and the reaction by the theatre community are documented in Wir Treten Aus Unseren Rollen Aus (Berlin: Zentrum für Theaterdokumentation und-information, 1990). Students and faculty from the *Hochschule für Schauspielkunst* participated in these events and are cited in the text.

as an institute of higher learning in the Federal Republic of Germany (*FRD*) beginning with the 1990 winter semester. A lengthy analysis was conducted in 1991 by the Council of Sciences concerning the integration of educational institutions of the new German states (*Neue Bundesländer*) into the *FRD*. The viability of many programs was questioned and many were merged with other similar institutions or eliminated completely.[12] The *HfSK* was recommended to continue in its entirety. In the report the Council of Sciences cited the tradition of the *HfSK* as being well known throughout Germany and Europe noting,

> The training at the *Hochschule* is recognized (lit.) "from all over," therefore it should be continued as it is....With only 150 students it is the smallest *Hochschule* in Berlin; continuance as an independent *Hochschule* despite it's small size is due entirely to the quality of education, the special educational goals, and special requirements.[13]

Based upon the recommendations of the Council of Sciences, the Berlin Parliament (*Berliner Abgeordnetenhaus*) granted the *HfSK* independent status. This high vote of confidence allowed the *HfSK* to handle all of its affairs internally; no longer under the auspices of governing bodies such as the Ministry of Culture and the Academy of Arts. The Council of Sciences would, however, conduct yearly audits. The Parliament recommended that the *HfSK* receive funding for 200 students, inclusive of all programs. Fifty new students could be accepted on a yearly basis.[14]

As a whole, the core of the program of study at the *HfSK*, with its emphasis on training for the German repertory system, was little affected by German Reunification. Obligatory seminars in areas such as Marxism/Leninism and World Economy were eliminated. No new theoretical classes were added; those blocks of time were replaced with additional hours of practical instruction in acting, speech and

---

[12] Of the theatre schools eliminated or merged the most notable was the *Staatiche Schauspielschule Rostock*. Many other dance and music schools, such as the *Fachschule für Tanz* in Leipzig, were eliminated.

[13] Wissenschaftsrat: Empfelungen zur künftigen Struktur der Hochschullandschaft in den neuen Ländern und im Ostteil von Berlin, Teil I (Köln: Herausgegeben vom Wissenschaftsrat, 1992), p. 218.

[14] Ibid., p. 217.

movement. Practically all the professors interviewed for this study were of the opinion that the acting program had changed very little. Change of a greater magnitude came with the influx of western students and the resultant change in student attitudes. There was no longer an emphasis on political issues and providing theatre for workers. The mixture of students from a variety of political and economic backgrounds resulted in occasional conflicts of ideology, but the overall feeling was a new freedom of expression. Students were more open to political dialogue and artistic criticism.[15] Because the *HfSK* was incorporated into the *FRD*, new relationships could be established with countries from the West. Beginning in 1990, several co-productions were arranged with the major theatre school from West Berlin, the *Hochschule der Künste* (*HdK*), at the *studiotheater BAT.* Additionally, in spring of 1991 an exchange was arranged with the Eugene O'Neill Theater Center in the United States. In May 1991 fourteen students from the *HfSK* traveled to Waterford, Connecticut to the Eugene O'Neill Center for a three-week seminar and, along with the students from the Center, received instruction in performing in American musical theatre and contemporary American drama. Traditional and contemporary American drama was performed and discussed with scenes ranging from A Streetcar Named Desire to The Normal Heart.[16] The following month the entire group traveled to Berlin (Schöneweide) to the *HfSK* to study German classical and contemporary theatre. The focus was on plays by Schiller, Goethe, Kleist and Büchner as well as Brecht and Heiner Müller. The entire two-month workshop was concluded with a

---

[15] This information comes from several sources. Professors who made statements in this regard include Ulrich Engelmann, Eva-Marie Otte, Kurt Veth, and Veronica Drogi.
[16] Kurt Veth, Berlin, Germany, May 1993.

performance of selected scenes and musical numbers at *Amerika-Haus* in West Berlin.[17]

Since 1990, the *HfSK* has gained greater access to western literature and plays. In the GDR, educational institutions were not, in theory, denied access to world literature. Professor of acting Ulrich Engelmann stated that studio performances of "questionable" plays were only discouraged, not forbidden. The greatest danger one might face, according to Engelmann, was a "slap on the hand" if cultural authorities became aware that formalist material, such as Beckett and Ionesco, was being utilized. Engelmann noted that the real problem was getting access to western literature and drama. Translations of avant-garde plays and other literature designated as "formalist" were generally only available through West Germany, and were neither published nor available for purchase in the GDR. Nevertheless, copies of unapproved works were available in virtually all the state libraries, in addition to works that were smuggled into the GDR.[18]

After 1989 western scholars were allowed greater access to the *HfSK*. This was also true of other former East German institutions, as Americans have also visited the *Theaterhochschule "Hans Otto"* in Leipzig.[19] My written request to visit the *HfSK* was approved in June 1991. The remainder of this chapter will document what I observed at the *HfSK* in May 1992 and May 1993.

Theatre Training in 1992-93

---

[17] Information documenting this event came from three sources - interviews with Kurt Veth of the *Hochschule für Schauspielkunst*, an informal phone interview with Jane Percy of the Eugene O'Neill Theater Center, and an information sheet distributed by the *Hochschule* entitled "Student Exchange - *Hochschule für Schauspielkunst 'Ernst Busch'* and National Theater Institute/Eugene O'Neill Theater Center, USA."

[18] Ulrich Engelmann, Berlin, Germany, May 1993.

[19] I was informed by Sylke-Kristin Deimig, Public Relations director of the *Theaterhochschule "Hans Otto"* that Paul Walker of the Acting Company (NYC) had been allowed to teach there as early as October 1991.

Facilities

The main campus of the *HfSK* is located in the center of the village of Schöneweide, approximately twenty miles south of downtown eastern Berlin. Schöneweide is a sleepy little village, quite unlike the more urban portions of Berlin, and seems a rather odd place to find a world class theatre training school. It is not a place frequented by tourists, nor does it have any distinctive businesses or shops. It seems to have remained as it was during the early years of the GDR: a rural, working class town removed from the dynamic energy of Berlin. When I arrived in 1992, I found that the main campus housed the acting program and consisted of a single large structure.[21] The exterior of the building is brick, and, like most edifices erected by GDR architects, the design suggests uniformity and impersonal functionalism. In order to enter, it was necessary to pass through a security clearance area that was staffed during all open hours. During my visits, I observed that security was tight; but, once they were aware of my purpose and recognized my face, I regularly passed without problem. Just inside the main entrance there is a lobby where students gather between classes and where audiences can wait prior to in-house performances. The *Studiobühne* (studio stage) *"Wolfgang Heinz"* is located just to the visitor's left past the security area, while the lobby is on the right. Prominently displayed in the lobby is a bust of the actor Ernst Busch.

Like the rest of the facility, the *Studiobühne* is not glamorous but is very functional. Plastic and folding chairs are placed on upward sloping levels, with a seating capacity of about 120. The auditorium arrangement is that of a larger "black

---

[21] There were two small buildings beside the main complex for storing properties and scenery.

[22] A black box is a flexible performing space, which can be set up in a number of configurations. Though the studio was arranged as a proscenium space in May 1993, it would be possible to arrange the seating into thrust, arena or environmental staging. All lighting occurred from above and there were positions for hanging scenic elements throughout the studio.

box."[22] The stage is large, about forty feet wide by fifty feet deep. During my visit, aged off-white curtains were hung as back drop and wing borders, though more for texture than for masking, as they were practically transparent. There were no overhead borders and all the machinery and equipment above could be seen. Additionally, most lighting instruments were in full view.

Proceeding into the building, the callboard was the next item of note. Students are instructed to check the callboard daily, as all room assignments, private voice class times and locales, and important messages are displayed and continually updated. There is a second area which lists all acting scenes being performed at the *HfSK* (when, where and by/with whom) and a final area which lists job opportunities, plays and workshops in progress throughout the Berlin area, and other activities of interest to the students. On the first level there is a studio for acrobatics and fencing classes, the library and archive, another large area for student gathering, and a small cafeteria (*mensa*). Behind the building which houses the *HfSK* is a large area called the *garten* (lit. garden), where students sit, talk, eat and relax between classes. It was the favorite gathering area for students during both of my visits, probably due to the lovely spring weather, which seemed to be the norm throughout May in Berlin. The library holds about 2,000 volumes, including playscripts, historical and theoretical works, and biographies. Included is a certain amount of archive material including a collection of videos of performances which have taken place at the *Studiobühne "Wolfgang Heinz"* and at the *studiotheater BAT*.[23] A reading area for students is also included, with several popular theatrical as well as non-theatrical publications available. The two upper floors are accessed by one of three stair units. Occupying approximately one-third of the second floor are the two main office suites, the

---

[23]Since these two terms occur in close proximity a note of explanation is needed. In all published material these are the accepted titles of these performing spaces - the *Studiobühne "Wolfgang Heinz"* and the *studiotheater BAT*. Quotations are commonly used when a structure is named after a person - Heinz was a former acting teacher at the State Acting Academy. In all print the word "*studiotheater*" was never found to be capitalized, but *BAT (Berlier Arbeiter's Theatre)* was printed in all capital letters.

Rektorate suite for the Rektor, Pro Rektor, and Chancellor, and the second for the Division of Acting. The larger suite of the Rektorate consists of two areas. The Rektor, Professor Dr. Klaus Völker, has a large office and an adjoining office occupied by his private secretary. The Pro Rektor, Professor Herbert Minnich, and the Chancellor, Caspar von Rex, each have private offices. A computer system, installed in November of 1992, is located in the small waiting area between the offices of the Pro-Rektor and Chancellor. The offices of the division of acting are located just down the hall.

The remainder of the second floor is taken up by the smaller *studiobühnen* where scene work and voice classes are held, and a few smaller offices for the professors. Only those with the rank of professor have private offices, while the remainder of the assistant professors and instructors handle their affairs through the office of the division secretary. There are eighteen of the smaller studio stages, all located on the second and third floors. These are the most distinctive features of the *HfSK*, as they are where most of the acting classes take place. There are always several studios available even during the busiest part of the day, so students have ample area for scene work classes, rehearsal, voice lessons, singing lessons, or private vocalizing. Each of the studio stages is equipped with a small wooden stage, which occupies about half the room. Small floodlights, controlled separately from the room's main lighting light the stages. Several of the stages have more elaborate theatrical lighting complete with small portable dimmer packs. Each has a few items of furniture and some were equipped with pianos.

On the third floor is the dance studio, named after the school's most famous dance professor, Hildegaard Buchwald-Wegeleben. It is a moderately sized studio, about twenty by sixty feet, with a mirror hung on one of the long walls. The studio contains an aged grand piano to provide accompaniment for the movement and dance classes. The floor is made of wood (seemingly, the original had never been replaced), and there are *barres* for ballet along three walls.

Included on the third floor is a substantial storage area where properties and costumes are checked out for use in scene work. Students can select costumes, accessories, and stage properties after the first read through of a scene, and the staff gathers the necessary items so that the students can have them for the first blocking rehearsal. The props and costumes are tagged and retained by the property manager, and prior to each scene work session, students are instructed to arrive early and retrieve them.

As I have stated before, the building struck me as not glamorous but very practical. There were no bright colors or vivid designs along the walls. Most of the interior was creme-colored and gave one the feeling of uniformity and the lack of individuality stressed by socialist doctrine. The overall atmosphere was very working class - a factory where actors are crafted.

Studiotheater BAT. One of the unique facets of the program at the *HfSK* is the *studiotheater BAT*. The *studiotheater* is located in Prenzlauer Berg, approximately ten miles north of Alexanderplatz in central East Berlin. The building was erected during the early days of the German Democratic Republic, and first utilized by the rebel balladeer, Wolf Bierman, who named the theatre the *Berliner Arbeiters' Theater* (BAT), or Workers' Theatre of Berlin. It flourished for over a decade; but as the worker's theatre movement began to wane the theatre was converted into a movie house. The *Institute für Schauspielregie* (also *Regieinstitut*), established in 1974, took over the building, and reestablished its original function as a playhouse. Initially an independent entity, the *Regieinstitut* was formally connected with the Schöneweide Campus in 1981 when it was granted *Hochschule* status.

The *studiotheater BAT* has maintained an active repertory of classical and new plays and features professional actors as well as student actors and directors. The theatre has one hundred thirty seats facing the stage on a very steep rake. The stage dimensions are approximately the same as the *Studiobühne "Wolfgang Heinz,"* and although the theatre has no fly system, very large drops can hang from the ample space above the stage. The theatre also features a scene shop and a computerized lighting system.

Adjacent to the theatre is a wing for faculty and business offices, and classrooms. There are three large classrooms utilized for seminars in theatrical design and directing classes, and also for rehearsals. There are six offices for members of the directing faculty, a business office, and an office for the personal secretary of Professor Peter Kleinert, director of the Directing program.

Theater am Park. The *Theater am Park* is a facility acquired by the *HfSK* in 1992 to give the choreography program a permanent home. The theatre is located on the grounds of the former Schöneberg military base, about forty miles southeast of downtown East Berlin. It was extremely difficult for me to find, and once found, very difficult to access. Guards at the gate asked many questions (even though I had an appointment), asked to see all material I was bringing in with me, and asked that no pictures be taken. The military base seemed to be at least partially operational, and, presumably, there was still some measure of secured data and/or materials within. They finally allowed me to take one picture, with their supervision, of the theatre's exterior.

The building has the same architectural characteristics that the main building in Schöneweide possessed. However, it seemed to have been abandoned for a few years, and was not in very good repair at the time of my visit. The large studio and dressing rooms, which are the only areas utilized by the choreography program has been adequately restored to meet the daily needs of the dancers and faculty. The main studio is very large, and is most likely a former basketball court converted into a dance studio. The size of the studio is approximately ninety feet square, and the roof is about sixty feet high. There are mirrors along one wall and several portable ballet *barres* which had been pushed to the side of the room. There are two main dressing rooms, one each for men and women. Each of the dressing rooms has an area for students to gather, talk, plan, and engage in other activities.

111

Curriculum

The *HfSK* seeks to provide practical training in the performing arts modeled on the traditions of German theatrical history. The goal of the school is to provide highly trained artists to perform in the best theatres in the German speaking world. More specifically, however, the instruction is based on the work of Konstantin Stanislavski and Bertolt Brecht. This philosophy was engendered when the school existed as the *Staatliche Schauspielschule*, and was still in place at the time of my visit. While there have been several philosophical changes since the disintegration of the GDR, the administration believes that the theories of Brecht and Stanislavski remain the most significant influences on the German theatrical tradition, and are, therefore retained.[24]

Though it is evident, as spelled out in the instructional bulletin, that the course of instruction has a solid theoretical base, each of the division leaders made one thing very clear to me: the students learn by doing. Only a very small percentage of the coursework is given over to theoretical concerns. In fact, it was not uncommon for professors to state "there is no theory, no method, just good solid acting!"[25] Clearly, the focus of the training is on *Handwerk* or the craft elements of acting. Therefore, acting, movement and voice classes constitute the bulk of the training program at the *HfSK*. Since the goal of the *HfSK* is to "continue to provide the best actors on the German stage," the administration is very secure with the fact that, for the last fifty years, they have trained almost all of the great actors who were, as of 1993, working in the major theatres of Berlin, as well as many of the best theaters throughout the German speaking world.[26]

<u>Acting</u>. The acting program at the *HfSK* is a four-year program (eight

---

[24]Klaus Völker, Berlin, Germany, May 1993.
[25]Ulrich Engelmann, Berlin, Germany, May 1993.
[26]Kurt Veth, Berlin, Germany, May 1992.

semesters of study), culminating in the conferral of an appropriate *Diplom*. Under the umbrella of the division of acting (*Bereich Schauspiel*), five distinct areas of study exist: acting, speech, movement for the actor, a smaller division of music (primarily singing), and a division of Theatre Science (*Theaterwissenschaft*), which includes classes in theatre history, dramatic theory, and dramatic literature. The program in acting has two parts. The first two years of instruction are known as foundational studies (*Grundstudium*). During this initial period, the student receives a thorough grounding in rules and principles through a series of lessons known as *Regelunterricht*. The students are divided into groups of ten to twelve for improvisation, groups of from two to four for more personalized instruction in acting (scene work), voice and music, and finally in groups of from ten to twenty for movement and dance classes. According to Wolfgang Rodler, head of the acting program, it is most important that students begin, in their first year of study, to learn the craft. Most of this happens through the voice and movement exercises, but they are also expected to learn to read, analyze, and perform scenes. Rodler stated: Yes, they can learn to simply recite words, etc., but the meaning, what is underneath it all, is what they must find. They must develop an appetite for discovering and showing human relationships. They must obtain a lust for playing.[27]

During the first semester of study at the *HfSK*, students are enrolled in a course entitled the *Improvisations-Seminar*, a class that has been in existence under various titles since the Reinhardt era. The course meets every day for four hours and, as the title suggests, students are expected to develop their skill at improvisation. It is perhaps in this course, that it is easiest to witness the direction of actor training taken during the years of the GDR. Throughout the seminar the dialectic between improvisation and fixation is explored. It is felt that the creative process, invented during improvisation, can only be captured when the actor learns to repeat it unmechanically, and therefore creatively. Only by repeating the improvisation to the

---

[27] Wolfgang Rodler, Berlin, Germany, May 1993.

point of fixation does the actor determine the direction of his overall process of production. This is realized through the creation of a process for improvisation, a process which later can be transferred to the creation of a role from a written text. The process has several aspects. First of all, the actor has to make sure that the improvisation is based on reality, not metaphorical or fantastical elements. Settings should be from the real world and problems should be dramatized in a psychological manner. Focus should be on practical activity, such as the handling of properties, but not as an end in itself. Props should be evaluated with respect to the actor's own being, with meaning and motives. An example is summarized below:

> A purse on a park bench. A student passes by, notices the purse, goes over to it, takes a hurried look around, picks up the purse, sits down, and quickly opens it. He pokes around in it, finds nothing, and, disappointed, lays it back down on the park bench.[28]

In the above example the process is this: the student attaches himself to an object. Elements of character come into being, as the student is viewed as a casual thief. A course of motivational action is developed as the student makes a series of decisions based on evaluation of a situation.

The process described is isolated as the basic rule of the seminar in improvisation - "observe-evaluate-react". If adhered to by the student actor, this formula provides the basis for concrete dramatic experience. Therefore this rule is insisted upon by the faculty of the seminar.[29] This simple formula has become one of the major creators of dramatic action.

Another important concept of the improvisation stressed in the seminar is the idea of a pivotal point. This is the point when the actor makes a discovery, is faced with the necessity to make a decision, and follows a course of action. Each pivotal point constitutes a block of action separated by the "observe-evaluate-react"

---

[28]Gerhard Ebert "*Lernen zu Improvisationen*" in Schauspielen Handbuch eds. Gerhard Ebert and Rudolf Penka (Berlin: Henschel Verlag, 1988), p. 4.

rule. The changes of action at pivotal points are the result of decisions, or of new attitudes toward the situation. Therefore the dialectic between attitude and action becomes the smallest building block of the actor.

Finally, the idea of self-projection onto a character is highly discouraged in the seminar in improvisation. Students are not to confront situations at a personal level, but to experience them actively, and with a psychic awareness of the situation.[30] If confronted at a personal level, students will become stuck at the level of emotionality. This, in turn, inhibits their ability to play within the established situation, and brings their personal lives to the forefront. Instead, they are encouraged to play from within a generalized, or archetypal self.[31]

According to Daniel Morgenroth, one of the leading actors at the *Deutsches Theater* who studied at the *HfSK* from 1986 until 1990, the class is divided into groups of ten to twelve students, each group under one of the major acting professors. They begin by sitting around and discussing situations that they have either witnessed or taken part in. They then divide into groups, which take turns reenacting the scenes and serving as the audience. Students not only become more adept at improvisation, but also develop and utilize their skills of observation.[32] Later in the semester, they move into discussing situations in certain plays[33] and, without actually reading from the script, work their way into extended improvisations based on their own experiences and imagination. Morgenroth stated:

> We did this for three months, but as it developed we got closer and closer to an actual play. But not with the text of the play, with our own text...with the discoveries of how our own text and the situations related to us.[34]

---

[29]Ibid., p. 6.

[30]Kurt Veth, Berlin, Germany, May 1992.

[31]Gerhard Ebert "Lernen zu Improvisationen" in Schauspielen Handbook eds. Gerhard Ebert and Rudolf Penka (Berlin: Henschel Verlag, 1988), p. 15.

[32]Daniel Morgenroth, Berlin, Germany, May 1993.

[34]Daniel Morgenroth, Berlin, Germany, May 1993.

In the second semester the students continue with their established group and leader, and move to performing scenes from actual texts on which their discussion and improvisations were based. They also begin to perform scenes in smaller groups of two to four, working with other instructors to accomplish this. In the second semester students are responsible for two scene study projects, and one *Wahlrollenstudium*[35] project (a role of the students choice). For the scene study projects they are assigned partners and instructors, and worked on the scenes for four hours a day, two days a week. With the *Wahlrollenstudium* project they are required, with the assistance of an instructor, to select a role that they hope to perform. After the selection is made, the student and the instructor meet for four hours a day twice weekly and work on the role. They begin by discussing and analyzing the role and performing improvisations. Later, monologues are selected and rehearsed and, in most cases, a partner is brought in for scene work. All work is done in full costume and with sets and properties from the first rehearsal. Scene study and *Wahlrollenstudium* projects last for six weeks each. At the end of each session, the projects are performed for a panel of judges who decide whether or not the student "passes," meaning that the project is deemed acceptable. As is usually the case with artistic projects, including those from schools in the United States, the decision basically consists of a judgement call on the part of the committee. They merely state that the project is acceptable or not and outline their reasons for the decision. In the event that a student does not pass, he or she will be required to repeat the project, perhaps with a new instructor, new material, and/or a new partner. After two failures, the student could be asked to leave the program.[36]

As indicated earlier, during the second semester students begin to work

---

[35]Since there is no covenient way to word this in English within the body of the text, the German will be maintained.

[36]Professor Veth told me in 1992 that only on rare occasions have students been failed or removed from the program. The few instances he could remember were students who decided on other careers. Failed scenes are more common, but these are usually personality conflicts and are resolved by assigning alternate partners and/or instructors.

on short scenes from plays. Those scenes are generally assigned by the faculty members and are drawn from the contemporary theatre.[37] Scenes are selected on the basis of the needs and desires of the individual students, and as a response to the following question: "what should we play - for whom - and why?"[38] In the context of the education of an actor, the question "for whom" has a different context than it would if the artistic director of a major theatre company asked the question. The "for whom" is related to the students, their needs as developing actors and actresses, their personal problems and productivity. The text itself is to contain a large amount of *Assoziationsmaterial*, or material that the student has some basis for understanding. Ideally, the material would be drawn from the present-day, with, at least in the beginning of a students study, everyday common occurrences as action. This allows the students to master simple actions in a recognizable environment before moving on to more complex actions from other periods. They learn, in conjunction with the improvisation seminar, the process for building action (observe, evaluate, react), as well as to explore the continuum between fantasy and discipline, and between spontaneity and fixation.[39]

During the second year the students are expected to have developed their speaking and movement skills to the point where they display a level of artistry. The voice should be well supported, and able to carry the highest emotional content required by the best of world drama.[40] Their bodies should display a high level of development. Traits such as strength, flexibility, and the ability to commit fully to even the most strenuous physical requirements are expected from them. According to Professor Rodler, "Second year actors must be filled with possibilities." They should have developed trust and, more importantly, confidence in themselves and their

---

[37] Occasionally the students made strong requests for scenes and these were considered.

[38] Gertrud Elisabeth Zillmer "*Aufbruch*" in Schauspielen Handbuch ed. Gerhard Ebert and Rudolf Penka (Berlin: Henschel Verlag, 1988), p. 163.

[39] Ibid., p. 164.

[40] Klaus Klawitter, Berlin, Germany, May 1993.

technique. The goal is that they can place an interesting character on the stage. In the fall semester of their second year, students take a second improvisation seminar and are also responsible for two scene study projects and one *Wahlrollenstudium*.

In the second year, scenework is taken primarily from three types of dramatic literature: Greek classics, Shakespeare and his contemporaries, and German classics (i.e. Lessing, Goethe, Schiller, Kleist, and Büchner). By this time, the students have had several months of experience with the recitation of classical literature via individual sessions with their vocal coaches. The emphasis in the second year is that students move outside their own realm of experience and imagine the given circumstances of characters and periods different from their own. According to Kurt Veth, former Rektor of the institution:

> ...the actor should not worry about whether the problems or circumstances are possible for him. This is not interesting for me. You must find the character, the character of King Lear. There are many possible situations that an actor has not yet experienced, and these are best, because it is not interesting to see the personal problems of an actor or actress on stage. That has nothing to do with art. When I go to the theatre, I want to see a bird (sic) that is comparable with my bird, but it cannot be my bird. Then I can look at the two and compare the realities.[41]

Years three and four, or semesters five through eight, are known as *Hauptstudium* (primary, or chief studies). During this portion of the training, they are gradually weaned from the daily individual contact with professors and are forced to begin to think for themselves. At this point much of the actual training ceases, a major point of contention for some students.[42] The reason for this is simple: the final two years are project based. Students are assigned to various projects, ranging from scenes, to acts of plays, to full-length works. Each student is assigned a mentor, who monitors their progress and gives them feedback, works with them individually,

---

[41] Kurt Veth, Berlin, Germany, May 1993.

[42] Several students, who preferred to remain anonymous, expressed this view. This will be discussed in greater detail in chapter seven.

handles complaints, and encourages their progression. In addition, the faculty of the division of acting meets once weekly, with one of their topics of discussion being student progress and problems.

Many of the third year students are cast immediately at the *studiotheater BAT*, while, for others this does not happen until the fourth year. This is generally determined by casting needs, but occasionally a student is kept off the stage because he or she needs remedial work in one or more areas. Scene projects are much longer, including entire acts of plays and one-acts. Students work in groups of from three to five, but most commonly they are placed in groups of four. The greatest difference between the scenes performed by students in the third year and those from the two previous years is even greater attention to detail. In May of 1992 I witnessed a rehearsal of a scene from Schiller's Intrigue and Love (*Kabale und Liebe*), performed three third year students under the direction of Kurt Veth. The students worked for two hours without a break on what seemed to be a two-minute cutting from the scene, addressing the subtext, and trying to locate stronger verbs with which to play the action. The students displayed an amazing ability to keep focused and committed to the work that had to be done. In a discussion with the students afterwards, I was able to glean some understanding of their intense focus. Quite simply, they realized that their time at the *HfSK* was short and that they couldn't afford to waste any time. They were confident that they would be working professionally afterwards and they wanted to be as prepared as possible for their future.

During the fourth year, the students continue to work in longer projects, and are often involved in several of the productions at the *studiotheater BAT*. Because the primary focus of the fourth year is rehearsal and performance of major projects, there are no actual acting classes required, though many drop in on various classes to observe or participate. At some point during the final year of study, each acting student has to perform a *Diplom-Projekt*, a final project consisting of a substantial role at the *studiotheater BAT*. The project, which in theory provides the ultimate testimony of the student's ability as an actor, is carefully coordinated between the student, his or her mentor, and the administration at the *studiotheater*. Because the *studiotheater* is a repertory company, plays remain in the schedule for two to three months. This affords the student many opportunities to perform the role, with their progress constantly monitored by their mentor and representatives from the division of acting.

Thus, the acting program at the *HfSK* is characterized by a very intense first two years of training followed by two years of gradually lengthening projects, culminating in a final project. As I alluded earlier, students are occasionally shocked and/or dissatisfied as much of the formal training ends after two years. Often, they feel neglected during the last two years, and do not continue to work at the same level as they were made to during the first two years. Others, however, find this to be an advantage. According to Thomas Mathys, a student from Switzerland:

> ... this is where the true *hochschule* attitude begins - with the freeness of instruction. During the last year what was required was a very sudden jump into self- sufficiency, due to the self-discipline that is required. For many it is too sudden, and there isn't really a smooth transition.[43]

Speech Training (*Sprecherziehung*). The program in speech and voice training exists solely as a support program for the division of acting, i.e., there is no focus on voice, or a program which develops future teachers of voice, though many eventually go elsewhere to obtain training as a *Sprechleiter*, or voice specialist. Long range goals of the program in speech training include a specialization in speech pedagogy and a *Diplom* offered for professional voice coaches.[44]

As of May 1993 there were eight full-time faculty members in the area of speech training, coordinated by Professor Herbert Minnich. The faculty arranges meetings with acting and directing students during slots of time between the larger

---

[43]Thomas Mathys, Berlin, Germany, May 1993.

[44]Herbert Minnich, Berlin, Germany, May 1993.

group classes (i.e. acting and dance). During the first year of study, each class consists of two students and one faculty member. Private lessons are given to each student for the remaining three years. Each student meets with his/her voice teacher three times weekly, for one hour, during the first two years. During the third year the schedule is relaxed to twice weekly, and finally to one hour weekly during the fourth year. Students are strongly encouraged to switch vocal coaches throughout their training in order to get different perspectives.

Though it is very taxing on the voice faculty to handle the large numbers of students in private lessons, it illustrates their commitment to one of their primary goals - to allow each student to find his or her individual voice.[45] It is felt that in large groups, it is difficult for students to hear their own voice sufficiently. Only through private, individualized instruction can students develop the desired subtleness and variety of vocal production. Additionally, student projects are frequently audio recorded and played back to the students as a means of self-evaluation.

Philosophically, Minnich and Klawitter contend that the basis of the speech program lies in the Brechtian theory of *gestic* language. *Gestus* in language has to do with a particular attitude adopted by the speaker towards others. Therefore the *gest* of a character determines his or her tone of voice, articulation, volume, facial expression and other characteristics of delivery. An actor's delivery should follow the *gest* of the character and acknowledge a change in *Gest*. The underlying idea by the faculty is that all physical activity, including vocal production, is controlled by the *Gest*. In other words, the voice should not simply be worked out for its own sake without relation to *gestic* activity of some kind.[46]

This, therefore, became the basis for training: allow the speech process to develop as part of the *gestic* through-line. The pedagogical process utilized by the faculty at the *HfSK* is three fold. Initially, students work with sounds and syllables,

---

[45]Klaus Klawitter, Berlin, Germany, May 1993.

[46]Herbert Minnich, Berlin, Germany, May 1993.

and undergo some elementary placement exercises to make sure their voice is well supported by breath. Then with a partner, they begin to work on *gestic* activity. This is accomplished by using the voice to frighten the partner, to seduce the partner, to send the partner away - in short, to motivate the use of the voice. The second stage in the process is to acknowledge the rest stage of the vocal mechanism and make use of it. In lectures to students, the voice is compared to a machine. According to Minnich, the most efficient machines maintain their activity through the rest stage as well as the working stage. Minnich cautioned the students not to always "force" their voice or overcompensate. Even in moments of high tension on stage the rest cycle is to be acknowledged. The final stage is the introduction of material into the *gestic* process. Primarily, classical texts are used by students from the outset of their training. Unlike the acting classes, it is felt that students should begin in their first year to work with difficult classical texts. There is a decided emphasis on the German classics, with works by Schiller and Goethe clearly emerging as the favorites.[47]

Speeches are broken down, sentence by sentence, into individual G*ests*. The actors work on the subtle changes between *Gests*, always with the idea of involving the entire body. In a vocal class with Margot Drevus, I was able to see this happen. A student had prepared Trinculo's speech (II.ii) from Shakespeare's <u>The Tempest</u>. Initially, Drevus had the student lie flat on his back and perform leg lifts, to sensitize the actor's midsection, as she put it. Then the actor was asked to say the syllable "wo" in a slow and elongated fashion. Next, the actor was told to play the *Gest*, or "physical subtext" of the monologue under the elongated syllable "wo," while still performing the leg lifts. This entire process was excruciating for the actor, who eventually was forced to use his entire body just to speak. After this process, the actor stood and began to perform the speech, utilizing the same amount of energy used during the floor work.

Vocal training at the *HfSK* is somewhat different than that in the United

---

[47] This was stressed by Kurt Veth, former Rektor of the *HfSK*.

States. Very seldom does one hear a great deal of "instrumentation" or tuning of the voice without relation to an activity or speech. Actors engage in simple articulation exercises, very much like that associated with Edith Skinner in American schools, during the initial stages of the training. Classroom time is eventually used for these exercises only briefly, if at all, in favor of work with text. Even then, the work on voice is not considered separately from the rest of the *gestic* process.

In addition to speech for the actor, each student is given a two-semester sequence in singing. The process involved is much like the process utilized for the speaking exercises, with emphasis on the *Gest*. Students are introduced to basic vocal exercises, then work on songs that are deemed appropriate. Material chosen is primarily from German composers like Weill and Eisler, but several students were working on German translations of American compositions by Rodgers and Hammerstein and Lerner and Lowe.

Movement (*Bewegung*). Movement classes in the *Grundstudium* portion of a student's training consist of three basic areas - acrobatics, dance, and movement for the actor. Each of the classes meets for one full semester for two days per week, one hour per class period. Classes take place in the Hildegaard Buchwald-Wegeleben dance studio and in a fully equipped studio for acrobatics and gymnastics. There are four full time faculty members in the area of movement, with other classes and workshops taught by guest professors and members of the Choreography faculty.

The philosophy of the stage movement program was developed by Hildegaard Buchwald-Wegeleben during the years of the German Democratic Republic at State Acting Academy of East Berlin. Primarily, the philosophy was developed in opposition to what stage movement classes had been in Germany prior to the mid-twentieth century - classes which taught posturing, gesticulation, and stylized movement on stage in an effort to be "aesthetically correct" and beautiful.[48]

---

[48]Hildegaard Buchwald-Wegeleben, "*Bewegung*" in Schauspielen Handbuch ed. Gerhard Ebert and Rudolf Penka (Berlin: Henschel Verlag, 1988), p. 199.

This style of movement began to prove useless as a training style for realistic art, which was not always beautiful and aesthetically pleasing. Professor Buchwald-Wegeleben began to look at the content of the plays themselves, to determine what kinds of skills were required of the actor. From her investigation, she determined:

> ...only with highly developed bodily capabilities can the actor meet the demands of the plays. For our purposes, it is important we take the actor to a level that he can learn certain more advanced skills quickly. For example the sabre dance of Eilif in <u>Mother Courage</u>, the fencing scene in <u>Romeo and Juliet</u>, the acrobatic feats of Truffaldino in <u>Servant of Two Masters</u> and so on...[49]

Both of the movement faculty members that I interviewed, Eva Marie Otte and Vera Neumann, studied at the State Acting Academy under Professor Buchwald-Wegeleben. Both attested to the influence that Professor Buchwald-Wegeleben had on their careers and both utilized her basic methodology in their classes. The basis of the method is this: the concrete motivation and association of each movement to action. In the same way that the voice faculty claims not to teach "voice for voice's sake," the movement faculty does not teach movement for movement's sake. Throughout the movement classes, students are constantly forced to relate their movement to concrete situations. For example, in Neumann's stage movement class, a simple movement pattern is established - walking for four counts, followed by two jumps, a one count pause and a clap, giving the students an eight count phrase. The students copy the phrase several times until they knew it well. Then Neumann introduces attitudes, such as scariness, happiness, anger, etc., and asks the students to perform the movement with the added state of being. These types of exercises are continued throughout the class, always with the idea of a state of being or objective in mind. Other exercises include slow motion "carving" movements through space with the arms, with different styles of music introduced. Students are

---

[49]Ibid., p. 200.

asked to interpret the music while utilizing the carving gestures. To complement the actor movement classes, students are given a second area of movement each semester. First year students take a two-semester course in acrobatics consisting of basic tumbling, balancing, and fitness. During this sequence they cover elementary stage combat exercises and beginning gymnastics. As with the acting classes, students are encouraged to work with props, and to establish a motivation for all movements. During one of the classes that I witnessed, students were practicing ladder falls. After a short scene was improvised, one actor chased the other up a ladder and during a mock fight the ladder began to fall. The students had learned how to fall to the side of the ladder and roll to ensure a safe landing. The goal of the acrobatics classes is to build the students strength and flexibility during the first year so that they move easily into the more advanced styles of movement.

Second year students take a two-semester course titled *Tanz*, which covers a variety of dance forms. Students are given instruction in basic ballet during the fall semester, with less emphasis on strict form and more emphasis on freedom of expression. In Otte's dance class that I observed, students began, after a brief stretching session, to perform simple jumps, straight up and down, similar to ballet jumps known as *echappe saute*.[50] Students performed the same jumps, but with a different energy as different styles of music were introduced. These classes were very basic, when compared with similar ballet classes in the United States, and the German students appeared to have had little formal dance training.[51] In the spring semester of the second year students continue with basic balance and conditioning work. Additional areas, such as period movement are covered. Later, in Otte's dance class, the students were shown pictures of Renaissance characters and architecture, and

---

[50] These are simple jumps straight up in the air from first position. The goal is not to jump too high, but to be able to point the toes before arriving back on the ground.

[51] In comparison with ballet classes I had taken at the University of South Carolina, the University of Colorado, and at professional studios like the Miami Ballet, these classes were technically very simplistic. It must be stressed that these classes were not for dancers, however but for actors with little or no dance training.

were asked to move around the room while the accompanist played Renaissance music. After allowing the students to create for themselves, Otte then displayed some basic movements from the period, including arm posturing, bows, curtsies and standing positions. She explained the restrictions placed on movement by period costumes and how this influenced the mannerisms and movement style. This may sound simple, but I was told that students in this class were only given a brief "feel" for the style of each period.

During the *Hauptstudium* portion of a student's training, they are given specialized instruction in several different areas. Students move into more advanced classes, such as stage combat, stage fencing, advanced dance, tap dancing, and dancing for musical theatre and opera. Because of the project-oriented nature of the *Hauptstudium*, students are often introduced to particular skills as needed, and during the final year of study, they have the option of skipping formal movement classes altogether.

Theatre Science (*Theaterwissenschaft*). Throughout the history of the *HfSK*, a great deal of emphasis has always been placed on historical and theoretical coursework. However, the shift from socialism to a unified capitalist Germany has greatly reduced this area of study. Students are no longer given seminars in Marxism-Leninism, World Economy, and Social Science. According to the Rektor, Klaus Völker, the ideological part of the education has completely disappeared.

During each semester of the *Grundstudium* students are offered a course in Theatre Science. First year students are given a two-semester course in theatre history, similar to what one would find in the United States. The basic difference is that students are not tested during the course. Standardized tests are administered prior to the student's entrance into the *Hauptstudium* portion of their training. Also, unlike most theatre schools in the United States, no text is utilized. Students are given a bibliography at the outset of their studies and are expected to have read the necessary materials before the administration of the standardized tests. These tests, administered in March of each year, are conducted by a representative of the *Prüfungscommission* (Examination Board).[52] Second year students are offered a course which focuses on the nineteenth and twentieth century theatre and theatre personalities, primarily in Germany. In this course the basis of Stanislavski's method is covered, as well as theories of Brecht, Meyerhold, Strasburg and other acting/performance theorists. These discussions serve as an overview of the theories, to solidify the students grasp of these concepts and to clarify misunderstandings. Additionally, the lives of famous German actors and actresses are traced and their performing methods discussed.

<u>Directing</u> (*Regie*). The directing program at the *HfSK* is located at the *studiotheater BAT*, described previously in this chapter. Students in the program develop plays for production and attend most of their academic classes at the studiotheater and adjoining classrooms. Classes in theatre science are occasionally conducted at a nearby seminar room in Prenzlauer Berg and, during the first two years of study, directing students attend acting and voice classes at the Schöneweide campus.

There are four full-time professors in the directing program, with Professor Peter Kleinert serving as division leader. Many adjuncts are employed, several of whom have been guest directors at the studiotheater. Students are accustomed to working with internationally known directors such as Robert Wilson, Heiner Müller and Andrea Breth.[53]

As of 1993 there were 25 students in the directing program. Entrance standards are very high, with six to eight students accepted each year from three to five hundred applicants. During my association with the school, the entire student

---

[52] Klaus Völker, Berlin, Germany, May 1993.

[53] A third year directing student, Christopher Roos, was selected by Robert Wilson to work on his production of <u>Doctor Faustus Lights the Lights</u> at the *Hochschule* in 1991. Several years earlier, directing and acting students worked with Heiner Müller in his 1988 production of <u>Der Löhndrucker</u> at the *Deutsches Theater*. In 1993 students were given a week long seminar by Andrea Breth, one of the resident directors of the *Schaubühne am Lehniner Platz*.

group of the directing program was comprised of German Nationals. In order to be accepted into the program, students must undergo a process similar to that of the acting students. After a written application is filed, approximately one-third are selected to audition.[54] Those selected must arrange to travel to Prenzlauer and perform a standard acting audition.[55] In addition, they must bring to the audition a completed scene analysis of a pre-assigned play to discuss with the assembled faculty of the directing program. The entire audition/interview process for each applicant lasts about two hours.

Kleinert informed me that the bulk of the program consists of practical theatre work. Though there are many courses offered which deal with theoretical issues, Kleinert stressed the fact that they are only interested in theoretical issues as revealed through practical theatre work. Most courses had practical requirements; for example, the required course in *Bühnenbild* (scenic design) required the student to work on the scenic crew of at least one production at the studiotheater, in addition to required classroom activities.

For the first two years of the program, the *Grundstudium* or foundational studies, directing students are required to take a basic directing seminar, during which they develop scenes among themselves. Each student director is assigned a mentor who assists the student in scene and cast selection, and who guides the student through the rehearsal and performance process. Scenes are presented to the directing faculty who make recommendations as to whether or not the student passes, or must repeat the project. Each student is also assigned as an assistant director for one of the mainstage productions at the *studiotheater BAT*. The requirements of the directing program are quite demanding, which probably explains the relatively high rate of attrition among first and second year students.[56]

---

[54]Peter Kleinert, Berlin, Germany, May 1992.

[55]See description of acting program for details regarding audition process.

[56]According to Kleinert, on the average one student drops out per year.

Those who make it into the *Hauptstudium* portion of their training are responsible for directing longer scenes in preparation for their diploma project - a full-length play at the *studiotheater BAT*. Third year directors utilize third and fourth year acting students for their projects, while fourth year diploma projects consist of a mixture of third and fourth year students and professional actors hired by the *studiotheater*.[57] Kleinert noted that all directing students had to test their skills on professional actors before leaving the program.

Choreography (*Choreographie*). The choreography program is the most recently developed program at the *HfSK*, having begun in 1988. As of 1993 there were 18 students in the program, with four or five new students selected each year. The faculty of the choreography program consists of two full-time professors: the director of the program, Dietmar Seyffert, and Holger Bey. I was told that other faculty members are hired as needed on an adjunct basis. A graduate of the Leningrad School of Art, Seyffert has served as resident choreographer of the *Deutsche Staatsoper* for eight years and in 1993 was one of the resident choreographers at the *Komische Oper*. Additionally he has directed at the *Burgtheater* in Vienna, the *Semper Oper* in Dresden, and at the *Leipzig Oper*. He has directed, choreographed and taught all over the world including Denmark, Switzerland, Mexico, Japan and the United States.[58] For many years, Seyffert has served as a judge for several international ballet competitions.

Most students who enter the program were or have been established dancers for many years. This, however is not a requirement for the program. In fact, Seyffert himself stated that some of the best choreographers were not dancers, but

---

[57]The *studiotheater* contracts actors at the basic rate of between 1000 and 1250 *deutsche marks* weekly. The system at the *studiotheater* can be likened to that of an URTA guest artist situation in the United States.

[58]Professor Seyffert had choreographed productions for the Washington Ballet, San Fransisco Ballet, and in 1988 was a guest faculty member at the Baltimore University Art department

[59]Dietmar Seyffert, Berlin, Germany, May 1993.

were artists with exceptional visual insight. He cited individuals with backgrounds in painting, lighting design, and sculpting as being among the best choreographers he had known. Additionally, he stated that choreography projects need not be limited to dancers. Seyffert stated that one can choreograph with lights, dogs, trees, in short - with anything that can move.[59]

Courses in the choreography program are drawn from a wide variety of sources. Students are given basic dance classes, music theory, aesthetics, theatre history, copyright laws and many other courses. Each semester the students are responsible for choreographing one major project, using their fellow students as dancer/actors. They are also required to serve as dancers for other students' projects. For the diploma project the HfSK hires professional dancers.

Despite the relative youth of the program, a high rate of placement had already been achieved with all four 1992 graduates receiving contracts. Students had been contracted by the *Semper Oper* in Dresden, the Free Dance Theater of Berlin, the Nicosea Company in Cyprus, and with the Gira Company in Thüringen.[60]

---

[60]Ibid

CHAPTER 6

ACTORS PRESENT AND PAST - STUDENT PERSPECTIVES OF THE
HOCHSCHULE FÜR SCHAUSPIELKUNST
"ERNST BUSCH"

Student Body

From 1951 until 1981, only students from the GDR were accepted to study at the State Acting Academy of East Berlin, or any of the other state acting schools. Once the conversion from State Acting Academy to *Hochschule* took place in 1981, students from all over the world could be considered for acceptance. However, in most cases this was only allowed through official exchange programs, or through German scholarship foundations. From 1981 until 1994 (the time when this study was completed), less than ten percent of the student body was or had ever been comprised of students from outside of the Germanic region (inclusive of Germany, Austria, and Switzerland).[1] This is the case at practically all German institutions of higher learning. Because the institutions are state supported, a high priority is given to German nationals. Only a small percentage of German-fluent foreigners are permitted regular matriculation in German universities and *Hochschulen*. Tables 7.1 and 7.2 offer a complete breakdown of the student body in the acting division for the academic years 1991-92 and 1992-93. Acceptance into the

---

[1] This information was supplied to me directly from the Hochschule on an *Informationsblatter* (information sheet) entitled "Vorauswahl für Studiengang Schauspiel für Wintersemester 92/93." The information sheet supplied statistics regarding ratio of foreign students and German Nationals, including a breakdown of how many students were from the former Eastern and Western portions of Germany. Because there was no efficient method of record keeping before German unification, there are no records like this available for the years prior to 1991. General statistics quoted are based on interviews conducted with former Rektor Kurt Veth (1992) and current Rektor Klaus Völker (1993).

acting program, as the figures suggest, has been extremely difficult, particularly considering the increase in applicants from outside the former GDR. The directing program normally accepts six new students each year, while the program in Choreography accepts from four to six.

Table 6.1

1991-1992 Applicant/Acceptance Rate

Number of applicants	1102
Allowed to audition	625
Accepted	30
Men	40%
Women	60%
FDR	57%
GDR	37%
Non-German Nationals	6%

Table 6.2

1992-93 Applicant/Acceptance Rate

Number of applicants	1306
Allowed to audition	481
Accepted	30
Men	41%
Women	59%
FDR	57%
GDR	38%
Non-German Nationals	5%

The number of applications to each of these programs varies, but averages from three to five hundred each.[2] There is no program in technical theatre or theatrical design associated with the *HfSK*.

There are no specific rules which determine who gets accepted into the acting program. Obviously the primary factor is talent, but there are other considerations. Professor Veronica Drogi stated that she considers it essential for students to possess a measure of flexibility in their approach to acting. For example, at the required audition for the program, she allows the student to perform his/her prepared selections in their entirety before she makes any comments. Next, regardless of the student's performance, she will instruct them to perform the pieces differently - based on suggestions that she makes - in order to challenge the auditionee to see things from another perspective. Professor Drogi noted that students from the former eastern portion of Germany were much more rigid and inflexible than those from western Germany and abroad. She stated that she understood the rigid, dogmatic attitude of those from the East, but admitted that she had grown tired of what she defined as many former Easterners apparent resistance to new ideas. She said that she was more likely to recommend a candidate for acceptance who was receptive to suggestions.[3] Members of the voice faculty stated that they generally recommended students for acceptance who displayed proper vocal technique at the time of the audition. Professor Minnich cited such characteristics as proper placement, diction, and breath support as the desired qualities. A student's potential was cited as a consideration, but only if that meant the possibility of improving from good to excellent, not from mediocre to good. Other factors such as imagination, physical fitness, and knowledge of world theatre were listed as determinants.[4] Therefore, in

---

[2]Interviews conducted with Peter Kleinert, head of the Directing program, and Dietmar Seyffert, head of the program in Choreography, in Berlin, Germany, May 1993.

[3]Veronica Drogi, Berlin, Germany, May 1993.

[4]Interviews from a collection of faculty members, including Ulrich Engelmann, Wolfgang Rodler, Kurt Veth, and Eva Marie Otte, Berlin, Germany, May 1993.

the acting program the audition was the most important aspect of the application process. The directing faculty more closely scrutinized academic backgrounds, and a dance audition was required for the choreography program.

All students attend the *HfSK* for the same basic reason - in order to become a working theatre professional in Germany. As part of a survey that I conducted in May 1993, acting students were asked why they chose to study at the *HfSK* as opposed to some other theatre school in Germany. Of those surveyed, all students who responded said that they came to study at the *HfSK* because it had the reputation of being the best in the German-speaking world. Approximately half of those who responded were interested in the school's acting methodology, with its emphasis on Stanislavski and Brecht. Foreign students tended to be particularly attracted to the work of Brecht, since it is difficult to receive adequate training in Brecht's acting style outside of Germany.[5] Among German students, some simply wanted to study in Berlin as opposed to Leipzig or some other city in Germany.

It is difficult to classify what comprises an average student at the *HfSK*. Initially, it should be pointed out that the ratio of women to men at the Hochschule is approximately sixty- percent women to forty- percent men. In general, the students are older and academically more mature than American undergraduate college students. First year students at most German institutes of higher education are in their mid-twenties.[6] Primarily, this is due to the standard nine years of coursework required for the *Abitur*, roughly the German equivalent of a high school diploma. The coursework for the *Abitur* is rigorous, with the accent placed on either the humanities or sciences. Direct preparation for university and higher educational institutions is provided by a two year extended secondary school, the *Erweiterte Oberschule* (*EOC*), mandatory for those who wish to attend a *Hochschule* or a University. By

---

[5] Jeff Burrell. Berlin, Germany, May, 1993.

[6] This information is based on several sources. Most students interviewed were in their mid- to late twenties. Data from Matley's dissertation (Wayne State 1978) also supports this claim.

the time a student completes his/her secondary education, they are purportedly on the same level as an American graduate student, both in terms of age and maturity.[7]

As mentioned earlier, German students at the *HfSK* appear to take their education more seriously than do American students. Based on the classes that I observed, the students maintained their concentration throughout the four-hour acting classes without becoming apathetic or requesting breaks from the professor. While many of the students admitted to me that they were not completely interested in what their instructor had to say, they felt it important that they listen and appear attentive at all times. It is interesting to compare this information with Matley's observation concerning West German actor training programs almost twenty years ago. He stated:

> If there is one word that characterizes the German student it is seriousness. He is serious to the core about his work and his study. The American concept of the university being a playground and experimentation station for a percentage of the students simply doesn't apply in West Germany.[8]

Students at the *HfSK* are not nearly as interested in health and physical fitness as are their American counterparts. Characteristic of European society, most students appeared to bathe infrequently, neither men nor women shaved regularly, and most were not interested in the latest clothing styles and fashions. Few students seemed to get much exercise, aside from the required movement and dance classes, and almost all of the students smoked heavily. Nevertheless, in acting and movement classes they approached their work with a high level of physicality. They were less concerned with cultivating a pleasant looking image than with revealing the real heart of the characters they played. Given the fierce competition for openings at the school, a prospective student must now have enormous talent and/or very good internal

---

[7]Bruce Matley, "A Description and Evaluation of Professional Actor Training in the West German Public Acting Schools of Hannover and Essen." Ph.D. Dissertation. Wayne State University, 1978, p. 93.

[8]Ibid., p. 93-94.

connections. In fact, all students accepted into the acting program in 1992 and 1993 had some if not several years of performing experience. Youth theatre groups are common in German secondary schools, and were particularly important as teaching tools in the secondary schools of the German Democratic Republic.[9] Students cited groups such as *Laienspielengruppen* (amateur theatre groups) and *Schultheaters* (school theatres) as common early theatrical experiences. Several students currently at the *HfSK* came from famous German performing families. One example from the 1993 student body was Pierre Besson, third year acting student and son of famous East German director, Benno Besson. One third of the students who responded to the questionnaire had transferred from another German acting school.

Student Perception of the Acting Program

As part of the questionnaire that was distributed, current students were asked to evaluate the strengths and weaknesses of the program. Former students working professionally as of 1993 were also asked to supply comments regarding positive as well as negative aspects of the training at the *HfSK*. While many students requested that their responses to these questions be kept confidential, others did not feel the need to remain anonymous. Where it is appropriate names are given and citations listed.

The most often mentioned positive aspect of the training program was the attention to *Handwerk*, or craft, i.e., the tools needed by a actor to perform their craft - voice, movement, and acrobatics, among others. The hours of personal attention in voice class were listed as most beneficial, but movement skills such as fencing, dance, and tumbling were also cited.

Students were in agreement that the first two years of the program, in particular the *Improvisation Seminar*, were of the utmost importance. Thomas

---

[9]Daniel Morgenroth, Berlin, Germany, May 1993.

Mathys of Switzerland stated that during the seminar, the instructors worked with him to develop his performing personality, forcing him to make strong yet personal choices. Jeff Burrell, of the United States, said that the focus on improvisation as a "thinking act," (i.e. observe, evaluate, react) was most useful for later training in acting.

When asked if they felt they were being well-prepared for their careers, the current students gave primarily positive responses, and recognized that there was only so much that could be accomplished in four years. Any negative aspects were prefaced by statements such as "there is no such thing as a perfect school."[10]

Concerning the less satisfactory aspects of the school many students felt that the training *per se* essentially stopped after the first two years and many had trouble adjusting to the abrupt change. Although they recognized the independent, project-oriented nature of the *Hauptstudium*, students said they had trouble maintaining the techniques that they had been taught during the first two years. Another problematic aspect of the program, mentioned by one student, was the fact that one worked with too many instructors throughout the program. Given the variety of different approaches, it was confusing for the student-actor. Many were displeased with the movement training they received. Students stated that they would have liked more dance training, in particular - jazz and tap dancing. From an observer's viewpoint it was clear that the area of movement was the weakest at the *HfSK*. It was especially obvious when compared to movement classes at the *Hochschule der Künste* in western Berlin, where students were given more challenging classes in stage movement, ballet, jazz and tap dancing.[11]

---

[10] Matthias Bundshule, Berlin, Germany, May 1993.

[11] This is a personal observation. Students at the *Hochschule der Künste* (*HdK*) are given more movement training and the overall approach to acting is much more movement oriented. In addition there is a musical theatre curriculum at the *HdK* with professional level dance training.
Movement/dance training at the *Hochschule für Schauspielkunst* is primarily for actors who have not had dance training.

The great tradition of the school was viewed by students in both a positive and a negative manner. Several students mentioned that being a graduate of the "Ernst Busch" school was likely to help them get their first job, and that by attending the school they were becoming part of a rich tradition of German actor training. Others viewed the tradition as a myth, and felt that the school promoted the Brecht/Stanislavski ideas but in reality taught something different.

Employment Prospects

Given the changes that have occurred in German theatre between 1989 - 1993, many students have to face the hard reality of unemployment in the theatre profession. Diminishing subsidies and greater reliance on box office revenues are forcing companies to curtail acting and technical personnel in order to balance their budgets. Attendance fell sharply during this period in many theatres in the former GDR; the *Volkstheater Rostock*, which once had 2,000 subscribers, had only 300 in 1992.[12] Many theatres in Berlin, most notably the *Volksbühne* and the *Berliner Ensemble* experienced severe financial hardships due to reduced subsidies and loss of audience due to higher ticket prices. Both theatres scaled down their resident companies and imported several shows yearly from other European resident theatres in order to cut expenses. The *Deutsches Theater*, constantly viewed as the finest theatre of the GDR, was forced to hike prices due to diminished subsidies and experienced a drop in attendance from their normal 76% to 30% as of 1990.[13] As of 1992 there were 69 professional acting companies in the former GDR, as opposed to

---

[12]Barry Daniels, "Humpty Thespis Sat on a Wall: A Great Fall for East German Theatres?" Western European Stages (Spring 1991), p. 63.

[13]Yvonne Shafer, "Interview with Dieter Mann: From the DDR to Reunification" Western European Stages Vol.4: 1 (Spring 1992): 15.

[14]Kurt Lennartz, gen. ed., Theater in der DDR: Vom Aufbruch zur Wende (Velber: Erhard Friedrich Verlag, 1992), p. 68.

nearly one hundred in 1989.[14] Nevertheless, students from the *HfSK* seemed optimistic about their chances for employment when I spoke with them in 1993. In actuality many students begin working professionally as early as their second year of study. Arrangements are made for these situations between the student, the theatre and the *HfSK*, but professional activities were encouraged by the *HfSK*. A listing of students from the 1993 school year and the professional companies where they gained employment appears in Appendix 4.

For students in the *Grundstudium* long range projects were generally not possible, and employed students had to make up projects and/or classes missed. Students in the *Hauptstudium* benefited from much greater flexibility, and many students have managed to collect several impressive acting credits. In October of 1991, by invitation of former Rektor Kurt Veth, Robert Wilson traveled to Berlin to stage a workshop production of Doctor Faustus Lights the Lights with seven students from the *HfSK*. The production, performed at the *Studiotheater bat* in 1991, was considered a successful collaboration by both the *HfSK* and Wilson, and was then taken to several major European locations including Munich, Vienna, Milan and Hamburg.[15] Later the production appeared in New York City, as part of Lincoln Center's *Festival of Serious Fun* July 7-30, 1992. Additionally a student from the directing program, Christopher Roos, was selected by Wilson as his assistant director. In April 1993 the *HfSK* co-sponsored a production of Heiner Müller's Anatomie Titus Fall of Rome at the *Hebbel Theater* in western Berlin. All four actors in the production were acting students at the *HfSK*.

Despite the post-unification problems in German theatre, Kurt Veth estimated that approximately 80 percent of students from the *HfSK* obtain a contract with an acting company the first year after graduation.[16] Although the administration

---

[15] Kurt Veth, Berlin, Germany, May 1992.
[16] Ibid.

was unable to offer me precise statistics to document their claim, several professional actors from major Berlin theatre companies in 1993 agreed with this estimate. Actors at the *Deutsches Theater* were quick to point out that more members of their almost eighty person ensemble received their training at the *HfSK* than at any other institution.[17] Company listings from the 1992-93 season revealed that a majority of the actors in three of Berlin's most important theatres were trained at the *HfSK*. The resident company of the *Berliner Ensemble*, made up of 60 actors/actresses, included 26 graduates of the *HfSK*, with two of the four full time directors being former faculty and/or students. At the *Maxim Gorki Theater* there were 31 actors/actresses with 19 having graduated from the *HfSK*. Both full time directors were former faculty/graduates, and 4 of 6 guest directors were faculty/graduates. At the *Deutsches Theater*, with a resident company of 72 actors in 1992-93, 32 were found to be graduates of the *HfSK*. Additionally two of the four resident directors were former faculty members. While the actual number of students in three of Berlin's most important resident theatre companies revealed a figure somewhat lower than that reported by the administration and former actors, it did suggest a very high success rate for former graduates; especially considering the fact that the theatres profiled were three of the finest in Germany.[18]

Former Students - Reactions to the Program of Study

Dieter Mann. Mann studied at the State Acting Academy of East Berlin from 1962 until 1964. Like many, Mann was able to secure an acting contract with

---

[17] All four actors that I interviewed, Dieter Mann, Daniel Morgenroth, Christine Schorn, and Frank Lienert, supported this claim. Similar support was provided by Angela Gützkow, Superintendent of DT Service.

[18] Information obtained in Deutsches Buhnen Jahrbuch (Hamburg: Genossenschaft Deutschen Bühnenangehörigen, 1992), p. 64-71. The cast lists were cross referenced with a listing of graduates through the year 1987 that I obtained, so there are most likely some omissions. Unfortunately, the administration has not made it a policy of keeping accurate listings of student employment.

a professional theatre, the *Deutsches Theater*, during his final year of study. As of 1993 he had spent his entire professional career, over thirty years, at the *Deutsches Theater*. From 1984 - 1990 Mann served as *Intendant* of the theater; after those six years he returned to acting. During his thirty year association with the *Deutsches Theater*, Mann has played countless leading roles, including Truffaldino in The Servant of Two Masters, Tempel in Nathan the Wise, Julian in Der Turm, Ariel in The Tempest, and Edgar Wibeau in The New Sorrows of Young W. Additionally, he has appeared in approximately ninety films for the *DEFA* or television.

Before studying at the State Acting Academy, Mann had very little experience in theatre. This was common in the early years of the GDR, as most young people who were unable to attend a university sought specialized, vocational training - which included training for the theatre. Mann worked in a factory, making bolts and screws before becoming interested in theatre. As a factory worker, he was able to obtain theater tickets cheaply, so he became an avid theatregoer. This inspired him to audition for the program at the State Acting Academy.

Following his training, Mann's initial years at the *Deutsches Theater* Mann quickly made him one of the most popular actors in Berlin. Critics cited him as "a clever and flexible realistic actor - the prototype of what the State Acting Academy had been producing for over sixty years."[19] Mann certainly fit the desired model, coming to acting after having worked in a factory and symbolizing the "worker's consciousness" of the GDR. He later served as secretary of the Free German Youth, or *FDJ* (*Freie Deutsche Jugend*), and became active in political affairs. Later Mann would say (reflecting a Brechtian influence),

> If actors do not go on stage in order to discuss something of political concern, to touch the nerves of society, then the job is ruined and the theatre becomes nothing more than a culinary temple.[20]

---

[19] Gerhard Ebert, Schauspieler Werden in Berlin (Berlin: Berlin-Information, 1987.), p. 169.
[20] Ibid., p. 168.

According to Mann, the most important aspect of the State Acting Academy was the fact that almost 80 percent of the faculty members with whom he studied were theatre professionals. Friedo Solter, one of his acting teachers, was instrumental in helping Mann obtain his first contract at the *Deutsches Theater*. Since then, Solter and Mann have collaborated on dozens of productions. Mann cited other influences, such as Rudolf Penka and Hildegaard Buchwald-Wegeleben, as providing him with and approach that was both intellectual and highly athletic.

Mann stated that it is important that for a student to be exposed to both practical and intellectual training as well as to different, often contradictory acting approaches (i.e. Stanislavski, Brecht). At the Academy Mann was exposed to Marxism and Leninism, Bloch and Nietzsche, which gave him insight into the plays of Brecht and other playwrights of the GDR. For Mann, it was important that the training be kept broad, with the student forced to fill the gaps himself. Mann stated, ...for me, this was the greatest benefit, that I did not learn one specific approach to acting, as some actors do--they are only Brecht actors or Stanislavski actors. I was trained in several different approaches. As a comparison, the king of sport for me is the decathlon, not the ten-meter race. I don't think that an actor can be broadly enough trained from an aesthetic stance, an intellectual stance, or from a political stance. He must understand different approaches.[21]

<u>Christine Schorn</u>. Schorn's career mirrored Dieter Mann's. Like Mann, she was a student of Friedo Solter from 1962-64 and was contracted by the *Deutsches Theater* during her last year of study. Her first role at the *Deutsches Theater* was opposite Dieter Mann in *Unterwegs* (<u>On the Way</u>) by Heiner Müller. Like Mann, 1994 represented her thirtieth year at the *Deutsches Theater*. She had performed over

---

[21] Yvonne Shafer, "Interview with Dieter Mann: From the DDR to Reunification" <u>Western European Stages</u> Vol.4:1 (Spring 1992): 15.

sixty roles at the *Deutsches Theater* including the title role in James Joyce's Molly Bloom and Aase in Peer Gynt.

       Schorn also came to the theatre with a strong belief in the worker's movement. In her early teens she worked in a laundromat and later in clothing sales, auditioning for the State Acting Academy at age 16 in 1961. For Schorn the most important aspect of the academy was the seminars in Marxism/Leninism. This, according to Schorn, gave her the necessary information to create her characters on a social level. She said,

> Today's actors have very little conception of what it is like to be a worker. They go to school, then begin acting. We had to learn society first, both practically and theoretically, before we started recreating it.[22]

       Her greatest influences were, like Mann's, Friedo Solter and Rudolf Penka; but she stated that the school itself was an important influence. She cited the schools atmosphere and its socialistic emphasis as being "so beautiful from a philosophical nature." For her, the grounding in Marxism/Leninism, and its emphasis on the material world, provided her with a logic upon which she could construct roles.

       Frank Lienert. Lienert studied at the State Acting Academy from 1976 until 1979. During his final year of study he was placed at the *Maxim Gorki Theater* where he worked for three years. From 1979 until 1981 he acted at the *Volksbühne* and from 1981 until 1992 he was a member of the ensemble at the *Deutsches Theater*, and at the time of my interview with him (1993) he was performing at both the *Deutsches Theater* and the *Maxim Gorki Theater* in the capacity of a guest; directing studio productions at the *Deutsches Theater*; and teaching at the *HfSK*. Throughout his career Lienert had played a variety of leading roles including the title role in Goethe's Faust at the *Volksbühne* in 1981, and at the time he was performing the role of Guildenstern in Heiner Müller's Hamlet/Maschine and several smaller roles in the

---

[22]Christine Schorn, Berlin, Germany, May 1993.

highly successful adaptation of Hofmannsthal's *Der Turm* (The Tower), both at the *Deutsches Theater*. Lienert said that his greatest influences at the *HfSK* were Ottofritz Gaillard, Rudolf Penka and Thomas Langhoff. More than anyone else that I spoke to, Lienert was able to offer first hand information regarding Rudolf Penka's method of actor training. Initially, Lienert noted that Penka did not attempt to separate the personality of the student from his or her acting work. As has been noted previously, the initial year of training included much work on the actor's personality. Once the actor gained complete trust in his/her ability to make viable choices on stage, then the process was transferred to a dramatic script. According to Lienert, the encounter which made drama come to life was: "I am the material, and I tie myself up with the character, and it becomes personal."[23] When asked how the theories of Brecht fit in, Lienert stated that even though Brecht asked the actor to "show" a character, he (Brecht) was interested in the personality of the actor, and that within the actor there were possibilities which may or may not contradict those of the character. The resultant encounter, within the actor himself, brought about the beginnings of dramatic action. Lienert also acknowledged that, as in America, interpretations of Stanislavski have evolved in Germany as well. He noted that initially Stanislavski was associated with feelings more than action, and that only in the late 1960s and early 70s was the emphasis shifted to physical action.

Lienert stated that the most positive aspect of the training program was the use of external instructors, professionals from the Berlin area, to teach acting classes. He felt that this prevented a type of "glass house" effect from occurring, as was the case in the early days of the GDR. During his years as a student he was able to work several times with Thomas Langhoff, who took over the role of *Intendant* at the *Deutsches Theater* in 1991. His final project at the State Acting Academy, Urfaust, was directed by Langhoff, who subsequently helped Lienert obtain contracts with the *Maxim Gorki Theater* as well as the *Deutsches Theater*.

---

[23]Frank Lienert, Berlin, Germany, May 1993.

Lienert offered a unique perspective on the changes that have occurred at the *HfSK* since 1989. His response basically echoed that of the administration of the *HfSK*:

> The people have changed, the experience has changed, but the concrete work on the stage has not changed. Perhaps now there is an even greater sense of the individual's development through physical and vocal exercises. The heart of the program, however, has not changed.[24]

Lienert stated that his approach to teaching acting was based on the following philosophy:

> I decide the character; the character does not decide me. I decide what the character can and cannot do - he cannot do what he wants without me. I encounter everything, but with a sense of playfulness, of fantasy. The German word for actor dictates this - *schauspieler* - to play a show.[25]

Daniel Morgenroth. Morgenroth studied at the *Hochschule* from 1986 until 1990. During his last year of study he was also offered a contract with the *Deutsches Theater*, and as of 1993 he was still working there. Morgenroth had spent practically all of his career playing young "leading man" roles, like Frederick in Strindberg's The Pelican, Marquise Posa in Schiller's Don Carlos, and the title role in Ibsen's Peer Gynt.

Before attending the *HfSK*, Morgenroth acquired several years of performing experience in his youth. For eight years he performed in school theatre, finally quitting at age eighteen because of the extreme political control over the schools. Later he worked in a fringe theatre but got in trouble because of what he termed an "experimentation." Later, at age 22, he auditioned for the *HfSK*. Entrance was very difficult then, basically a one-in-fifty chance. Morgenroth noted that he had

---

[24]Frank Lienert, Berlin, Germany, May 1993.

[25]Ibid.

a great deal of confidence when he auditioned, and decided to take the attitude that he "knew that he would make it, and he did."[26]

Morgenroth was in the unique position of having attended the *HfSK* during the unification years. Even though he was at the *Deutsches Theater* for what would have been his last year of study, he was still very aware of changes that were taking place. He felt that from a student's perspective, the program changed a great deal.

> During the GDR there was more ideological control. For three days a week we had theoretical classes - four hours a day! Marxism/Leninism, Economics, there was too much of it. The balance was wrong. It is not needed in this profession. Things have changed and it is an advantage now. There is more focus on the acting.[27]

Having worked at the *Deutsches Theater* for three years, Morgenroth has seen the impact of the *HfSK* in terms of numbers of students working professionally. He said,

> It's crazy; in this ensemble most of the actors come from the *HfSK*. It is difficult to think of anyone who wasn't trained there. Oh yes - there are a few from Leipzig, but almost everyone came from the *Hochschule für Schauspielkunst*. It was the main school in the GDR and everyone wanted to go there. Leading directors would go there to teach and get the best actors. That was a real advantage.[28]

He noted, however, that there were areas in his training at the *HfSK* that were not adequately covered. Movement was, for him, the weakest area, and he would have liked more semesters and different styles of dance and movement training than he was given. Because he was fortunate enough to start working immediately at the *studiotheater BAT* during his third year, he missed additional movement and dance classes that he would have otherwise received. The strongest aspect for him was, in retrospect, the tradition of the *HfSK*. He respected the strong tradition,

---

[26]Daniel Morgenroth, Berlin, Germany, May 1993.

[27]Ibid.

[28]Ibid.

passed down from Reinhardt, to Penka, and then to the teachers of the present like Ulrich Engelmann. Morgenroth collaborated with Engelmann on his final project at the *HfSK* and later worked with him at the *Kammerspiele* of the *Deutsches Theater*.

CHAPTER 7

CONCLUSION

Evaluation of the *Hochschule für Schauspielkunst*

This study has examined the history of the *HfSK* and has analyzed the program of study, which was in effect at the *HfSK* during the years 1991 through 1993. The following evaluation of the *HfSK* will be based upon several criteria -- not solely on its success in preparing students for the profession of theatre. Placement may be considered only part of the criterion for an evaluation of the *HfSK*; during the years 1951 until 1989 the school had a 100% placement rate, as all graduates were guaranteed jobs in GDR state theatres. In order to broaden the perspective of the evaluation this concluding chapter will attempt to isolate factors in addition to job placement that will give the reader a clearer picture of the importance and future direction of the *HfSK*. Specifically, six questions will be addressed: 1) Has the *HfSK* been successful in preparing aspiring theatre students for careers in theatre? 2) Has the *HfSK* played a unique and important role in 20th Century German theatre?; 3) How has the *HfSK* reflected the changing political conditions of 20th Century Germany?; 4) How does the present program reflect the long tradition of actor training at the *HfSK*?; 5) How has the *HfSK* influenced/promoted the study and analysis of acting?; 6) What is likely to be the future of the *HfSK* in a unified Germany?

Has the *HfSK* been successful in preparing aspiring theatre students for careers in theatre? Since it has already been established that the *HfSK* has had

for careers in theatre? Since it has already been established that the *HfSK* has had a successful track record of placing graduates in professional theatres, it is important to investigate whether or not those students have been adequately prepared for their careers. Initially, it should be pointed that only the best are accepted into any of the fourteen official training programs, and entrance standards at the *HfSK* are among the highest. Students must have extraordinary talent, very good internal connections, or both. Once enrolled, the student has a good chance of becoming a professional actor, provided they finish the program. The approach taken at the *HfSK* is extremely practical; very little of the student's time is taken up by lectures and/or academic classes. They spend the first two years undertaking a rigorous curriculum of fundamental courses and the final two years developing a series of projects, culminating their studies with a final diploma project. Much of the fourth year can be regarded as an internship, as students perform within the repertoire at the *studiotheater BAT* or, on occasion, at another suitable theatre. Students make connections with professional directors and casting personnel while at the *HfSK*, and this usually determines where and when they begin to work as a professional actor.

Statistics in chapter seven revealed that close to 50% of the working professional actors in Berlin's three largest state theatres were trained at the *HfSK*, and many other graduates were working in large state theatres throughout Germany. According to the administration, the school has maintained about an 80% placement rate for first year graduates since the reunification of Germany in 1989.

Classes at the *HfSK* are kept small. Students are not trained *en mass*, as there is a great deal of personalized instruction -- particularly in the areas of acting and voice. Much of the work in acting is built around investigation of playscripts, i.e., the training is project-based and does not include a great deal of actor exercises which are not in some way related to performing pre-existing, text-based material. Voice training, while personalized and exploratory in nature, is also based on the performance of texts. The present administration at the *HfSK* is committed to producing individualized, self-confident performers as opposed to a mass of actors who have been formed into a particular model.

Given the high percentage of graduates of the *HfSK* working in professional theatres in Germany (particularly Berlin), and the corresponding use of professionals as instructors and directors of studio productions, the lines of communication between the training program and the intended places of employment have been very clear. In other words when a professional theatre hires a graduate of the *HfSK*, they are guaranteed a performer who speaks the same theatrical vocabulary that they do, and who has been trained by the best professional teachers and directors in Berlin. Graduates of the *HfSK* are confident, well-trained practitioners of the craft of theatre. Students at the *HfSK* did not display any doubt about their future careers. In fact, most believed that they had better work extra hard while in school in order to learn as much as they could before getting their first theatre job.

It seems, however, that there are improvements that could be made. For instance, the fourth year could be structured to include more required courses. This would not diminish or interfere with the student's theatre work, but allow the student the opportunity to continue to develop his or her craft in addition to the heavy performance requirements. Perhaps that activity would continue into more graduates' professional careers and allow them additional growth as artists.

As their incorporation into the FRG continues all of the former East German schools will be forced to include a more substantial academic component into the training program. At the *HfSK* this area seemed to be weak. Several students appeared to sleep through the required lectures and many neglected to take notes. Given the complexity of the German repertory and the theoretical nature of German performance aesthetics, it would seem that future theatre artists in Germany would greatly benefit from a more intensive offering of dramatic literature and theory.

Finally, the school itself was well overdue for renovation and/or additional construction. The facilities were merely adequate when compared to the

Hochschule der Künste in West Berlin and, presumably, most other schools from the former western part of Germany. This is not to say that these facilities would improve the training, but it would enhance the school's ability to continue to attract the best students.

Has the *HfSK* played a unique and important role in 20th Century German Theatre? Considering the Western world, there are only a handful of schools of theater which have managed to establish a real tradition of excellence. The *Conservatoire* of the *Comédie Française*, founded in 1786, has a long tradition of training actors, as does the school of the Moscow Art Theatre, established in 1909.[1] Cambridge and Oxford established dramatic societies in England in 1855 and 1856 respectively, and the Royal Academy of Dramatic Art was founded in 1904. In the United States the American Academy of Dramatic Arts, founded in New York City in 1884, is the oldest continuing program for training actors. The Yale School of Drama, established in 1924, also has a lengthy tradition of training theatre personnel. When looking at the Germanic region, certainly one must consider the *HfSK* with its legacy to the *Schauspielschule des Deutschen Theaters*, as having the greatest tradition. During the twentieth century the school has survived two world wars, and has existed under three names -- including a lengthy period as a major socialist school of theatre. However, the "Ernst Busch" school has displayed a resiliency in its adaptation to the various periods of German history. Throughout the often-confusing events of twentieth century Germany - Nazi Germany, the World Wars, the German Democratic Republic, and the now reunified Germany - the *HfSK* has maintained a high quality program for theatre training. With the number of actors working in major Berlin theatres and the statement made by professor Veth in 1992 that "all of the great actors then working on Berlin stages were trained at the *HfSK*," the impact of the school on the Berlin professional theatre has been enormous. With the exception of

---

[1] While the Moscow Art Theatre was established in October 1898, the first studio with Leopold Sulerzhitsky did not begin until 1909.

Marlene Dietrich, no former students from the school are well known in the United States; but in Germany, Austria, and parts of Scandanavia, many graduates have celebrity status. Dieter Mann is among the most famous of stage actors in Germany; Friedo Solter has been called one of the standard setting directors of the GDR[2] and in 1990 was still considered one of Germany's greatest directors. Like Mann, Solter had been associated with the *Deutsches Theater* for almost thirty years. Many other young actors, graduates of the *HfSK* were in 1993, performing in starring roles in Berlin. Ulrich Mühe, a 1968 graduate was playing the title role in Heiner Müller's internationally renowned Hamlet/Maschine at the *Deutsches Theater* and Daniel Morgenroth, a 1986 graduate was playing leading roles in Peer Gynt, Der Turm and The Pelican also at the *Deutsches Theater*. Götz Schubert, another 1986 graduate, was playing leading roles at the *Maxim Gorki Theater* and the *Deutsches Theater*. An analysis of one of the most popular shows at the *Deutsches Theater* during the summer of 1993, *Der Eismann Kommt* (The Iceman Cometh) revealed that out of the nineteen cast members, ten had graduated from the *HfSK*. An analysis of productions at the *Berliner Ensemble* and the *Maxim Gorki Theater* would undoubtedly yield similar results. With this large number of graduates appearing in major roles in major Berlin theatres, the school's influence cannot be denied.

Given the number of important directors such as Friedo Solter (*Deutsches Theater*), Thomas Langhoff (*Deutsches Theater*), and Rolf Winklegrund (*Maxim Gorki Theater*), all of whom were graduates and/or teachers at the *HfSK*, and the corresponding number of leading actors outlined above, it can be said that the genesis of the approach to acting on the Berlin stage has been the actor training program at the *Staatliche Schauspielschule Berlin/HfSK*. In interviews conducted

---

[2] Theatre in the German Democratic Republic, Volume 6. (Berlin: Center GDR of the International Theatre Institute, 1974.) p. 14.

by the author with several professional actors from Berlin, all mentioned professors from the *HfSK*, including Penka, Gaillard and Solter, as having the greatest influence on their careers.

How has the *HfSK* reflected the changing political conditions of 20th Century Germany? When Max Reinhardt founded the *Schauspielschule des Deutschen Theaters* in 1905, Germany was enjoying its greatest period of stability in history. Already with the strongest army in Europe, the Germans had begun, in 1898, to build what they hoped would become the strongest naval fleet as well. Arts and culture in Germany and Austria were recognized as among the best in Europe. Vienna's *Burgtheater* had long been considered one of Europe's finest ensembles while efforts by the Duke of Saxe-Meiningen had also brought international prominence to German acting. During the years after he took control of the *Deutsches Theater* in 1905, Max Reinhardt gained international prominence as a director. Concurrent with his rise to international fame, Reinhardt's *Schauspielschule* became known as one of the best in Europe. He had assembled a strong group of instructors who, in addition to their teaching duties, were working theatre professionals as well. Students undertook a wide variety of courses, but the most distinctive part of the program was their apprenticeship at the *Deutsches Theater*. The focus of the actor training in Reinhardt's school was the development the actor's physical and vocal technique, in order to produce actors who were capable of balancing the stage action against the large choruses employed by the great German director.

Reinhardt left Germany in 1933, though he had been primarily based in Austria since 1922, returning to Berlin sporadically until Hitler's rise to power made his departure necessary. The leadership of the *Schauspielschule des Deutschen Theaters* had been gradually passed over to Nazi sympathizers as early as 1931. After the Nazi takeover of Germany in 1933, the school was forced to adapt to Hitler's artistic demands, or it would have faced an earlier closing than it eventually experienced. Utilizing a bastardized version of the Stanislavski technique, actors were forced to endure long periods of intense psychological inquiry. Emotional memory exercises were used to probe the every detail of an actor's past, and to investigate the then current areas of his personal life. Delivery was modeled after Hitler's extended rhetorical speeches, and was named *Reichkanzleistil*. There were, however, those present in the school's organization who refused to comply with the Nazi authorities. Though they managed to maintain some of the program's integrity, their actions resulted in the closing of the *Schauspielschule* in 1943.

Wolfgang Langhoff was instrumental in the re-opening of the *Schauspielschule* in the summer of 1945 and was responsible for bringing back many of the teachers who had been forced out of the school during the Nazi years. Since he was *Intendant* of the *Deutsches Theater* at that time, Langhoff was able to maintain the school's strong connection with the professional theatre. The influence of Ottofritz Gaillard and Maxim Vallentin was felt throughout the latter years of the decade as all theatre schools in Germany began to recognize the Stanislavski method as the most suitable approach for realistic acting. In 1951 the school was designated as one of the three institutes of theatre training in the German Democratic Republic, was given a permanent site in Schöneweide, and was renamed the *Staatliche Schauspielschule Berlin*. Though the cultural hierarchy of the GDR labeled the Stanislavski approach as the only acceptable acting approach, the *Schauspielschule* was instrumental in the relaxation of those standards and with the gradual incorporation of the techniques of Brecht. The school's already high rate of placement (during the Reinhardt years) was raised to the level of complete placement of all graduates, as guaranteed by the GDR. Because of it's location (Berlin) and it's strong connection to the *Deutsches Theater* and other major Berlin theatres, the school became the "school of choice in the GDR" and continued to attract the most talented actors and teachers available.[3]

---

[3] Daniel Morgenroth, Berlin, Germany, May 1993.

How did the program of study, as it existed in 1992-93 reflect what can be classified as the "tradition of actor training" which had been developed by the *HfSK*? Several areas should be mentioned in this regard. Initially it should be stated that the *HfSK* had come full circle -- that is, it evidenced the same sense of eclecticism that Reinhardt had promoted when he opened the school in 1905. There was a growing sense of "westernization" during the time that this study was conducted (1992-93), which included a greater diversity in the literature that was performed, the styles of movement that were studied, and the greater diversity within the student population. Acting classes at the *HfSK* still evidenced the type of training one might have found at the school during the years of the GDR -- a strong realistic basis. In general students were required to dramatize situations from the real world utilizing material possessions from humankind's "world of things." The program was characterized by a variety of coursework -- one class, the improvisation seminar, had originated during the Reinhardt's tenure but had been somewhat modified during the GDR period. Most of the instructors who were in residence at the *HfSK* during my visits had taught during the years of the GDR and felt that the overall approach had changed very little. The focus of the program during the years 1992-93 was acting and directing in the realistic theatre. All instructors who were interviewed felt that it was most important for students to study the Stanislavski method initially and then to incorporate elements such as Brechtian theory later. By teaching the elements of both Stanislavski and Brecht, the administration of the *HfSK* felt that they covered the full range of performance styles.[4] **How has the *HfSK* influenced/promoted the study and analysis of acting**? Besides classroom study in the areas of acting, voice and movement, many of the faculty in applied areas have published extensively as well. Gaillard's <u>Das Deutsche Stanislavski Buch</u>, actually developed during his tenure at the *Deutsche Theatreinstitut* in Weimar, has been cited throughout this study.

---

[4] Kurt Veth, Berlin, Germany, May 1992.

Gaillard was associated with the *Staatliche Schauspielschule Berlin* for over ten years, publishing several more articles in addition to his book during that time. Rudolf Penka, associated with the *HfSK* for almost twenty years, published over a dozen articles during his lifetime in addition to teaching throughout Eastern Europe as a guest. A short full-length work entitled <u>Rudolf Penka: Versuch eines Arbeitsportraits</u> was published during his lifetime. Those associated with the HfSK have published numerous other articles, pamphlets and other materials. In addition, Gerhardt Ebert, an acting teacher and director who taught at the Staatliche Schauspielschule Berlin wrote two full-length books, <u>Schauspieler Werden in Berlin</u> and <u>Schauspielen Handbuch</u>. Klaus Völker, the Rektor in 1993, was at that time himself writing a book on the history of the *HfSK*.

Several of the professors from the *HfSK* have been guest directors and/or instructors at other theatres as well as theatre schools throughout the world. Rudolf Penka taught throughout communist eastern Europe, including Czechoslovakia, Romania and Hungary, as a guest instructor whenever his schedule permitted; Ulrich Engelmann, taught acting and directed in communist countries like Cuba, China and northern Korea; Kurt Veth was a guest teacher/director in Cairo, Egypt and at the *Mozarteum* in Salzburg, Austria; Dietmar Seyffert directed and choreographed in several countries including Russia, Japan and the United States. These activities were allowed on a restricted basis during the GDR years and allowed the school to extend its influence outside the primarily communist eastern European countries. **What is likely to be the school's future in a unified Germany?** It is difficult to predict what the future holds for the *Hoschschule für Schauspielkunst "Ernst Busch."* General recommendations from the Council of Sciences indicate that the strong connection of the former East German schools to professional theatres and the fact that the final year of study is spent in a studio theatre (such as the *studiotheater BAT*) could serve as a model for institutions in former West Germany. The Council stated,

> The *Wissenschaftsrat* sees no reason to recommend major changes in the structure of the theatre schools of the former eastern part of Germany. The

principal, that acting students become progressively incorporated into practical theatre work and complete their studies in a studio theatre, is exemplary, and should be retained.[5]

However, the Council also noted,

The education given at the theatre schools should be comprised of both practical and theoretical elements, and both should reflect a level of advanced study. Academic professors should be placed at the schools. In this regard, the usual scope of academic requirements would be broadened.[6]

By adding a stronger academic component to the curriculum the *HfSK* would more closely resemble schools of western Germany, but allow it to retain its strong practical foundation.

In a unified Germany the *HfSK* will face stiff competition for the best students. The *Hochschule der Künste (HdK)* which is located near downtown West Berlin presents a more centralized location to major theatres, far more plentiful and newer facilities, and a budget almost double that of the *HfSK*, and, presumably, higher pay for instructors. Increased attention to theatres in western Berlin, such as the *Schaubühne am Lehniner Platz* and the *Freie Volksbühne*, may make attendance at the *HdK* more attractive to the better students. Though their record of placement was not that of the *HfSK*, the administration at the *HdK* assured me that while their graduates often had to begin in the "provinces," more than 80% of all their graduates were also being hired their first year after graduation.[7]

Time and money may make for a more even playing field as far as theatre schools in Germany are concerned, but none will enjoy the great history that has been acknowledged in this study of the *HfSK*. But history is just that, schools of theatre and of other disciplines as well can only rely on reputation for a brief time. Concrete

---

[5]Wissenschaftsrat: Emphelungen zur Kunftigen Struktur der Hochschullandschraft in den Neuen Landern und im Ostteil von Berlin. Teile I-IV. (Berlin: Herausgeben vom Wissenschaftsrat, 1992), p. 202-203.
[6]Ibid, p. 203.

[7]Thomas Fragstein, Berlin, Germany, May 1993.

results bring students to both academic and vocational institutions. Only by adapting to a new set of circumstances in a unified Germany can the *Hochschule für Schauspielkunst "Ernst Busch"* continue to enjoy the same amount of recognition and success that it has previously experienced.

Suggestions for Further Study

Pedagogical research in theatre training presents a variety of challenges to those who wish to undertake it, particularly when conducted in a country other than their own. Differences in culture, language, and systemic organization are only modified by the cost of traveling abroad. However, the results can yield a deeper understanding of the process and of the theatre system of the country selected. That was found to be the case with my study at the *HfSK* - it became more than researching a school, it was the investigation of an educational tradition. Many of the professors who taught at the *HfSK* had themselves studied there. In America, that practice is occasionally referred to as "academic incest," but at the *HfSK* it is known as the preservation of a tradition of acting. The close integration of the school with the theatres of Berlin, both in terms of students and faculty, was of note. It would be useful to research one particular theatre, such as the *Deutsches Theater*, and investigate the tradition of acting maintained by the resident company.

There are other theatre training institutions in the Germanic region that would yield an interesting study, both from a pedagogical as well as a historical standpoint. The *Theaterhochschule "Hans Otto"* would undoubtedly rank first. Because it was created from the tradition of the *Deutsche Theaterinstitut Weimar*, the legacy of the Hans Otto School, it would include a more detailed study of the work of Maxim Vallentin and Ottofritz Gaillard, who founded the *Deutsche Theaterinstitut* in 1946. Similar results may be achieved in a study of the *Staatliche Schauspielschule Rostock*, although information about that program is very difficult to obtain. I received letters of invitation from both the *Theaterhochschule "Hans Otto"* and the *Hochschule für Musik und Theater Rostock* (loosely related to the *Staatliche Schauspielschule Rostock*), which indicated that there is a willingness on the part of the German institutions to participate in an exchange of knowledge regarding approaches to theatre training. A comparison of several of the German theatre schools would also be appropriate, but I found this to be financially prohibitive.

A study of the major film acting school of the GDR, the *Hochschule für Film und Fernsehen "Konrad Wolf"* would be a possible source for information regarding the training of actors and directors for film, as well as a comparison of the styles of acting utilized in German film and television. The *Hochschule der Künste*, which agreed to partial participation in my study, would provide an interesting pedagogical study of German acting styles, particularly if one were to compare the program at the *Hochschule der Künste* with that of the *Hochschule für Schauspielkunst "Ernst Busch."* It would be possible to undertake a study of the *Schauspielschule des Deutschen Theaters*, provided one could locate enough material for a dissertation length study. Additionally, it would entail several trips to Berlin, and close work with the staff of the *Deutsches Theater*.

As far as the various training methods in use in German theatre schools are concerned, there are many possibilities for additional study. It would be possible to compare the various approaches to acting used by any number, or perhaps all, of the fourteen institutions. This would be difficult both from the standpoint of accessibility and financial constraints, but would undoubtedly yield some interesting results. It would also be possible to undertake a broader sampling of graduates of the institutions, in order to arrive at a clearer picture of graduate placement. One must keep in mind that record keeping in the former eastern institutions (if the "Ernst Busch" is indicative) was very poor. Only in the early 1990s was computerization employed for recording data.

There are many aspects concerning the history of German actor training that would be served by closer study. It would be possible to undertake a more generalized overview of theatre training during the German Democratic Republic and to look at the evolution of training from 1949 to 1989. It would also be useful to study various systems of training in societies where actors are guaranteed employment yet given restrictions regarding artistic choices.

A study of the approach to vocal training in Germany is far overdue. In Bruce Matley's 1978 dissertation, cited frequently in this study, he suggested that someone investigate German approaches to vocal training. Almost twenty years later no one has attempted such a study. Though none of the voice coaches discussed the archaic concept of *Bühnensprach* (standardized stage speech/diction), all were employing standardized speech techniques in their classes. They were most interested in the Brechtian concept of *gestus*, and the use of a vocal "through line" or impetus for delivery. This approach would be well served by a complete study.

Several studies have been conducted regarding the theatre of the German Democratic Republic, but there is enough material available for many more. While playwrights like Heiner Müller and Volker Braun have been heavily studied, others such as Christoph Hein and Ulrich Plenzdorf have not. Plenzdorf's The New Sorrows of Young W. signaled the final downfall of socialist realism in the GDR, yet it is virtually unknown in the United States.

Finally, many of the teachers and other personalities that have been discussed in this dissertation would be best served by a full-length study. Foremost among those mentioned are Ottofritz Gaillard, Maxim Vallentin, and Rudolf Penka. Gaillard would probably prove most accessible since, at the time of this study, he was still living. Since each has influenced so many actors and directors who are still associated with the Berlin theatre, it would be possible to gain access to additional biographical material (other than that I have cited in this work) through interviews.

Due to the sheer volume of theatres and depth of the repertory, the German theatre system can arguably be considered the model of state-supported theatre. This system requires well-trained, versatile actors, skilled in a variety of theatrical styles and able to function well within a repertory system. In order to provide itself with a consistent influx of new talent, Germany has developed state-subsidized schools of acting, which, like the theatres they seek to replenish, can be considered models of a state-supported system for education in theatre. This study of one such program - the *Hochschule für Schauspielkunst "Ernst Busch"* has provided the reader with information and insight about the nature of theatre training in Germany.

APPENDIX 1

FACULTY OF THE HOCHSCHULE FÜR SCHAUSPIELKUNST "ERNST BUSCH" (1992-93)

Acting

Barbara Bismark
Ulrich Engelmann
Bernd Kunstmann
Christa Pasemann
Hans-Georg Simmgen
Kurt Veth

Veronica Drogi
Michael Keller
Uwe Lohnse
Wolfgang Rodler
Angelika Waller

Speech

Astrid-Angela Arnold
Klaus Klawitter
Herbert Minnich
Viola Schmidt

Margot Dreves
Karl Mickel
Cornelia Krawutschke
Monika Schneider

Movement

Horst Beeck
Eva-Maria Otte

Vera Naumann
Christof Walther

Directing/Choreography

Manfred Karge
Peter Schroth
Gero Troike

Peter Kleinert
Friedo Solter
Dietmar Seyffert

Theater Science

Wolfgang Engler+
Dieter Hoffmeier+
Ernst-Frieder Kratochwil

Klaus Greiner
Dieter Koppe
Klaus Volker

APPENDIX 2

HOCHSCHULE FÜR SCHAUSPIELKUNST "ERNST BUSCH"
LIST OF COURSES-DIVISION OF ACTING

First Year
Semester 1
Improvisation Seminar
Acting Fundamentals
Voice/Speech
Stage Movement
Acrobatics
Theater Science-History I

Semester 2
Scene Study (2)
Role of Choice (1)
Voice/Speech
Stage Movement
Acrobatics
Theatre Science-History II

Second Year
Semester 3
Improvisation Seminar II
Scene Study (2)
Role of Choice (1)
Voice/Speech
Voice Production
Stage Movement II
Dance
Theatre Science-Periods

Semester 4
Scene Study (3)
Voice/Speech
Voice Production
Stage Movement II
Dance
Theatre Science-Aesthetics

Third Year
Semester 5
Scene and Role Study
Voice/Speech-Special Projects
Singing
Stage Combat/Fencing
Project Work

Semester 6
Project Work and/or
studiotheater BAT project
Voice/Speech-Special Projects
Singing
Stage Combat/Fencing
Special Projects-Movement

Fourth Year
Semester 7
Special Studies
studiotheater BAT Project
Project Work
Diploma Project
Special Projects-Voice
Special Projects-Dance

Semester 8
Special Studies
studiotheater BAT Project
Practical Work
Professional Engagement
Special Projects-Voice
Special Projects-Dance
Diploma Project

APPENDIX 3

HOCHSCHULE FÜR SCHAUSPIELKUNST "ERNST BUSCH"
DIRECTING PROGRAM - LIST OF COURSES

First Year
(1-2 Semester)
Fundamentals of Directing
Fundamentals of Space
Methods of Acting
Voice/Speech
Stage Movement
Dramaturgical Analysis (Scene)
Scene Design I
*Theater Science
Assistant Director-BAT
Work with Professional Actors

Second Year
(3-4 Semester)
Advanced Directing
*Theater Science
Scene Design II
Text Analysis/Concepts
Scene Study (2)
Assistant Director-BAT
Assistant Director-Berlin Theater.
Stage Technology

Third Year
(5-6 Semester)
Dramaturgical Analysis (Play)
Director-BAT/Optional Theater
Directing Styles
Direction of Two Scenes (BAT)
*Theater Science
Directing Documentation
Lighting Design I, II

Fourth Year
(7-8 Semester)
Diploma Project
Project Documentation
Special Projects/Workshops
*Theater Science
Artistic/Technical Direction

a variety of seminars each semester are offered for directing students.

APPENDIX 4

1993 STUDENT ACTORS OFFERED PROFESSIONAL CONTRACTS

Second Year Students

Benjamin Utzerath	Schloßpark Theatre Berlin
Robert Kuchenbuch	Neue Bühne Senftenberg
Boris Aljinovic	Mecklenburg Staatstheater
Christian Schmidt	Hebbel Theater

Third Year Students

Matthais Bundschuh	Schauspiel Frankfurt
Weibke Kayser	Theaterdock Berlin/ Hebbel Theater
Barbara Seyffert	Theaterdock Berlin
Gabriele Völsch	Theaterdock Berlin/ Hebbel Theater
Tilo Mandel	Theaterdock Berlin/ Hebbel Theater
Heiko Senst	Theaterdock Berlin/ Hebbel Theater
Marco Bräutigam	Mecklenburgisches Staatstheater
Katrin Heller	Hebbel Theater
Thomas Lehmann	Hebbel Theater

Fourth Year Students

Katharina Waldau	Deutsches Theater/Theater Bonn
Dirk Audehm	Mecklenburgisches Staatstheater
Michael Günther	Mecklenburgisches Staatstheater
Bils Brück	Maxim Gorki Theater
Bettina Engelhardt	Deutsches Nationaltheater Weimar
Susanne Wagner	Projecttheater Dresden
Stephan Richter	Theater der Stadt Cottbus
Grit Riemer	Carrousel Theater

Bibliography

Anders, Friedrich. "Schauspieler Brauchen Wir." Theater der Zeit. October, 1951, pp. 4-5.

Bach, Steven. Marlene Dietrich: Life and Legend. New York: William Morrow and Company, 1992.

Bell Geddes, Norman. Miracle in the Evening. New York: Doubleday & Company, 1960.

Benedetti, Jean. Stanislavski. London: Routledge, 1988.

Bisztray, George. Marxist Models of Literary Realism. New York: Columbia University Press, 1978.

Boyle, Nicholas. Goethe: The Poet and the Age. Oxford: Clarendon Press, 1991.

Braun, Edward. The Director and The Stage: From Naturalism to Grotowski. New York, 1982.

Brecht, Bertolt. Brecht on Theatre. Translated and Edited by John Willett. London : Methuen, 1964.

- - - . Kleines Organon für das Theater. Frankfurt/Main: Suhrkamp Verlag, 1960.

- - - . Letters 1913 - 1956. New York: Routledge Press, 1990.

- - - . Über den Beruf des Schauspielers. Frankfurt/Main: Suhrkamp Verlag, 1970.

- - - . Über Realismus. Frankfurt/Main: Suhrkamp Verlag, 1971.

Brockett, Oscar. Century of Innovation. Boston: Allyn and Bacon, 1991

Brockett, Oscar. History of the Theatre, 5th Edition. Boston, Allyn and Bacon, 1992.

Buchwald-Wegeleben, Hildegard. "Bewegung" In Schauspielen Handbuch. Edited by Gerhard Ebert and Rudolf Penka. Berlin: Henschel Verlag, 1991, pp. 199-221.

Bundschul, Mattias. Student, *Hochschule für Schauspielkunst "Ernst Busch."* Personal Interview. May 1993.

Burrell, Jeff. Student - *Hochschule für Schauspielkunst "Ernst Busch"* : Personal Interview. May 1993.

Carlson, Marvin. Goethe and the Weimar Theatre. Ithaca: Cornell University Press, 1978.

- - - . The German Stage in the Nineteenth Century. Metuchen, N.J., 1972.

- - - . Theories of the Theatre. Ithaca: Cornell University Press, 1984.

Carter, Huntly. The Theatre of Max Reinhardt. New York, Bretano's, 1914.

Cole, Toby and Helen Krich Chinoy. Actors on Acting. New York : Crown Publishers, 1965.

Dennis, Mike. German Democratic republic: Politics, Economics, and Society. New York: Pinter Publishers, 1988.

Deutsches Bühnen Jahrbuch. Hamburg: *Genossenschaft Deutscher Bühnen Angehörigen*, 1992.

Devrient, Eduard. Geschichte der deutschen Schauspielkunst. Vol. I - V. Leipzig: Weber Verlag, 1848.

- - - . "Simplicity and Convention." In Actors on Acting. Edited by Toby Cole and Helen Krich Chinoy. New York: Crown Publishers, 1954, pp. 262-263.

Drogi, Veronika. Professor, *Hochschule für Schausipelkunst "Ernst Busch."* Personal Interview. May 1993.

Duerr, Edwin. The Length and Depth of Acting. New York: Holt, Rinehart and Winston, 1962.

Duke of Saxe-Meiningen, George II. "The Actor in the Ensemble." In Actors on Acting. Edited by Toby Cole and Helen Krich Chinoy. New York: Crown Publishers, 1954, pp. 263-267.

Ebert, Gerhard. Improvisation und Schauspielkunst: Über die Kreativität des Schauspielers. Berlin: Henschel Verlag, 1989.

- - - . "Lernen zu Improvisationen." Schauspielen Handbuch. Edited by Gerhard Ebert and Rudolf Penka. Berlin: Henschel Verlag, 1988, pp. 73-95.

- - . Schauspieler Werden in Berlin. Berlin: Berlin-Information, 1989.

Education and Training in the German Democratic Republic. Berlin: *Staatsverlag der Deutschen Demokratischen Republik*, 1966.

Edwards, Christine. The Stanislavski Heritage: It's Contribution to the Russian and American Theatre. New York: New York University Press, 1965.

Engelmann, Ulrich. *Professor, Hochschule für Schauspielkunst "Ernst Busch."* Personal Interview. May 1992, May 1993.

Flores, John. Poetry in East Germany: Adjustments, Visions, Provocations. New Haven: Yale University Press, 1971.

Fragstein, Thomas. *Rektor, Hochschule der Künste*, Berlin. Personal Interview. May 1993.

Gaillard, Ottofritz. "Aufgaben und Methoden." In Schauspielen Handbuch. Edited by Gerhard Ebert and Rudolf Penka. Berlin: Henschel Verlag, 1988, pp. 153-162.

- - - . "Neue Schauspielerziehung" Theater der Zeit December 1946: 36.

- - - . Das Deutsche Stanislavski Buch. Berlin: Aufbau-Verlag, 1947.

Gillespie, Gerald, Ed. German Theatre Before 1750. New York: Continuum Press, 1992.

Gerber, Margy, Ed. Studies in GDR Culture and Society: Selected Papers from the Tenth New Hampshire Symposium on the German Democratic Republic. Lanham, Maryland: University Press of America, 1984.

Gleiß, Jochen. "Spieler ohne Gefährten?" Theater der Zeit. September, 1991, pp. 12-15.

Goethe, Johann Wolfgang. "Rules for Actors." In Actors on Acting. Edited by Toby Cole and Helen Krich Chinoy. New York: Crown Publishers, 1954. pp. 248-256.

Gorchakov, Nikolai A. The Theatre in Soviet Russia. Translated by Edgar Lehman. New York, 1957

Gorelik, Mordecai. New Theatres for Old. New York: Samuel French, Inc., 1940.

Hayman, Ronald, Ed. The German Theatre: A Symposium. London: Oswald Wolff, 1975.

Hochschule für Schauspielkunst "Ernst Busch" Berlin: Information über die Hochschule und Ihre Bereiche. Berlin: Pressstelle der Hochschule für Schauspielkunst "Ernst Busch" Berlin, 1991.

Hoffman, Miriam. "Arbeit am Körper." Suddeutschen Zeitung, No. 114, May 1993, p. 49.

Huebener, Theodore. The Literature of East Germany. New York: Frederick Ungar Publishing Co. 1970.

Huettich, H.G. Theatre in the Planned Society: Contemporary Theatre in the German Democratic Republic. Chapel Hill: University of North Carolina Press, 1978.

Innes, C.D. Modern German Drama: A Study in Form. Cambridge: Cambridge University Press, 1979.

Kleinert, Peter. Director, *Regieinstitut*, Berlin. Personal Interview. May 1992.

Klunker, Heinz. "Theatrical Twilight in East Germany." Euromaske: The European Theatre Quarterly. Number 1, Fall 1990. pp. 13-18.

Kornfield, Paul. "Epilogue to the Actor." In Anthology of German Expressionist Drama, pp. 6-8. Edited by Walter Sokel. Ithaca, N.Y. : Cornell University Press, 1984.

Lamport, F.J. German Classical Drama. Cambridge: Cambridge University Press, 1990.

Lederer, Herbert. Handbook of East German Drama 1945-1985. New York: Peter Lang, 1991.

Lennartz, Kurt. Theater in der DDR: Vom Aufbruch Zur Wende. Sonderdruck: Erhard Friedrich Verlag, 1992.

Lienert, Frank. Actor. *Deutsches Theater*. Personal Interview. May 1993.

Matley, Bruce. "A Description and Evaluation of Profesional Actor Training in the West German Public Acting Schools of Hannover and Essen." Dissertation. Wayne State University, 1978.

Mann, Dieter. Actor, Deutsches Theater. Personal Interview. May 1993.

Mathys, Thomas. Student, *Hochschule für Schauspielkunst "Ernst Busch."* Personal Interview. May 1993.

Minnich, Herbert. Pro-Rektor, *Hochschule für Schauspielkunst "Ernst Busch."* Personal Interview. May 1993.

Morgenroth, Daniel. Actor, *Deutsches Theater*. Personal Interview. May 1993.

Osborne, John. The Meiningen Court Theatre 1866 - 1890. Cambridge: Cambridge University Press, 1988.

Otte, Eva-Maria. Professor, *Hochschule für Schauspilekunst*. Personal Interview. May 1993.

Patterson, Michael. The Revolution in German Theatre 1900 - 1933. London: Routledge & Kegan Paul, 1981.

Pietzsch, Ingeborg. "Am Anfang War Die Improvisation." Theater der Zeit. October, 1984.

Piscator, Erwin. "Objective Acting." In Actors on Acting. pp. 285-291. Edited by Toby Cole and Helen Krich Chinoy. New York : Crown Publishers, 1965.

Penka, Rudolf. "Arbeitserfahrungen mit Stanislavski und Brecht." In Schauspielen Handbuch. Edited by Gerhard Ebert and Rudolf Penka. Berlin : Henschel Verlag, 1991, pp. 35-40.

- - - . "Ein Heiratsantrug - Arbeit an Einer Szene von Anton Tscheckow." Stockholmer Protokoll: Aus der Arbeit der Staatliche Schauspielschule Berlin. Berlin: Henschel Verlag, 1969.

- - - . "Übergang zum Autorentext." In Schauspielen Handbuch. Edited by Gerhard Ebert and Rudolf Penka. Berlin: Henschel Verlag, 1988, pp. 138 - 150.

Piens, Gerhard. "Die Staatliche Schauspielschule Berlin" Stockholmer Protokoll: Aus der Arbeit der Staatliche Schauspielschule Berlin. Berlin Henschel Verlag, 1969.

Piscator, Erwin. "Objective Acting" Actors on Acting. Toby Cole and Helen Krich Chinoy, Eds. New York: Crown Publishers, 1965.

Reinhardt, Max. "The Enchanted Sense of Being." Actors on Acting. Eds. Toby Cole and Helen Krich Chinoy. New York: Crown Publishers, 1954.

Reinhardt, Max. Schriften. Berlin: Hugo Fetting, 1974.

Rodler, Wolfgang. Professor, *Hochschule für Schauspielkunst "Ernst Busch."* Personal Interview. May 1993.

Rouse, John. Brecht and the West German Theatre. Ann Arbor: University of Michigan Press, 1989.

Rudolf Penka: Versuch eines Arbeitsporträts. Berlin: Herausgeben vom die Hochschule für Schauspielkunst "Ernst Busch" Berlin/Deutsche Democratische Republik, 1983.

Russell, Douglas A. "The Visual Innovations of Max Reinhardt and His Designers" Modern Austrian Literature 18.2 (1985) : 21 - 30.

Sayler, Oliver M. Max Reinhardt and His Theatre. New York: Bretano's, 1924.

Schafer, Yvonne. "Interview With Dieter Mann: From the DDR to Reunification." Western European Stages Vol. IV, No. 1, Spring 1992.

Schneider, Eberhard. The G.D.R. The History, Politics, Economy and Society of East Germany. New York: St. Martin's Press, 1978.

Schorn, Christine. Actress, *Deutsches Theater*. Personal Interview. May 1993.

Scriven, Michael and Dennis Tate, Eds. European Socialist Realism. New York: St. Martin's Press, 1988.

Seyffert, Dietmar. Director, Choreographie Program, *Hochschule für Schauspielkunst "Ernst Busch."* Personal Interview. May 1993.

Socialist Realism in Literature and Art: A Collection of Articles. Moscow: Progress Publishers, 1971.

Sontheimer, Kurt and Wilhelm Bleek. The Government and Politics of East Germany. London: St. Martin's Press, 1975.

Speiss, Ron. Student, *Hochschule für Schauspielkunst "Ernst Busch."* Personal Interview. May 1993.

Stanislavski, Konstantin S. An Actor Prepares. New York: Theatre Arts Books, 1948.

- - - . Building a Character. New York: Theatre Arts Books, 1949.

- - - . Creating a Role. New York: Theatre Arts Books, 1961.

- - - . My Life in Art. New York: Theatre Arts Books, 1952.

Streisand, Joachim. Kulturgeschichte der DDR: Studien zu Ihren Historischen Grundlagen und Ihren Entwicklungsetappen. *Koln: Pahl-Rugenstein Verlag*, 1981.

Students and Colleges: Higher Education in the German Democratic Republic. Berlin: Panorama DDR, 1983.

Styan, J.L. Max Reinhardt. Cambridge: Cambridge University Press, 1982.

Subiotto, A.V. Bertolt Brechts Adaptations for the Berliner Ensemble. London: Modern Humanities Research Association, 1975.

Theatre in the German Democratic Republic, Volumes 1 - 7. Berlin: Center GDR of the International Theatre Institute, 1974.

Thomaneck, J.K.A. and James Mellis, Ed. Politics, Society and Government in the German Democratic Republic. New York: St. Martin's Press, 1989.

Veth, Kurt. Rektor, *Hochschule für Schauspielkunst "Ernst Busch."* Personal Interview. May 1992.

Voigt, Hans-Georg. "Arbeit an einer Szene unter Benutzung eines Modells." Stockholmer Protokoll: Aus der Arbeit der Staatliche Schauspielschule Berlin. Berlin: Henschel Verlag, 1969.

Völker, Klaus. Rektor (appointed October 1992) *Hochschule für Schauspiekunst "Ernst Busch."* Personal Interview. May 1993.

Wiles, Timothy. The Theatre Event: Modern Theories of Performance. Chicago: University of Chicago Press, 1980.

Willett, John. The Theatre of Bertolt Brecht. London: Methuen Press, 1967.

- - - . The Theatre of the Weimar Republic. New York: Holmes & Meier, 1985.

Williams, Simon. German Actors of the Eighteenth and Nineteenth Centuries. London: Greenwood Press, 1985.

Wir Treten aus Unserem Rollen Heraus: Dokumente des Aufbruchs. *Herbst* 1989. Berlin: *Zentrum für Theaterdokumentation und -information*, 1990.

Wissenschaftsrat: Emphelungen zur Künftigen Struktur der Hochschullandschaft in den Neuen Ländern und im Ostteil von Berlin. Teile I-IV. Berlin: *Herausgeben vom Wissenschaftrat*, 1992.

Zhadanov, Andrei A. "Soviet Literature--Richest in Ideas, the Most Advance Literature," In Dramatic Theory and Criticism: Greeks to Grotowski, edited by Bernard Dukore, 960-964. New York: Holt, Rinehardt and Winston, 1974.

Zillmer, Gertrud Elisabeth. "*Aufbruch*." In Schauspielen Handbuch, edited by Gerhard Ebert and Rudolf Penka, 138-150. Berlin: Henschel Verlag, 1991.

Index

A Midsummer Night's Dream (Shakespeare), 41, 42
A Streetcar Named Desire (Williams), 104
Abitur, 10, 134
Academy of Arts, 103
Ackermann, Konrad, 18
American Academy of Dramatic Arts, 153
Amerika-Haus, 105
Anchaz, Carl Ludwig, 63
Anatomie Titus Fall of Rome (Müller), 139
Aus den Erfahrungen des Sowjettheaters, 72
Ausschuss, 30

BaFög, 10
Bel Geddes, Norman, 45
Bergmann, Ernst, 53
Berliner Abgeordnetenhaus, 103
Berliner Arbeiters' Theater, 109
Berliner Ensemble, 3, 8, 108, 110-111, 140
Besson, Benno, 136
Besson, Pierre, 136
Bewegung, 122, 137
Bey, Holger, 128
Bierman, Wolf, 101, 109
Brahm, Otto, 33
Brecht, Bertolt, 2, 4, 6, 38, 40-41, 68, 75-77, 92, 96, 98-103, 108, 110-111, 115, 123, 141, 149
Breth, Andrea, 126
Buchwald-Wegeleben, Hildegaard, 100, 120, 122
Bühne der Jugend, 55
Bühnenschriften-Vertriebsgesellschaft m.b.H, 12
Bukharin, Nikolai, 73
Burgtheater, 30-34, 54, 128, 154
Burrell, Jeff, 137
Busch, Ernst, 2, 7, 16, 83, 96, 107-109, 117
Brockett, Oscar, 28

Caucasian Chalk Circle (Brecht), 108
Central Theatre Agency, 12, 81
Chronegk, Ludwig, 32
Circus Schumann, 44, 48, 57

Clausen, Claus, 57
Conservatoire of the Comédie Francaise, 2, 32, 54, 152

von Dalberg, Baron Herbert, 27
Das Deutsche Stanislavski Buch (Gaillard), 72-74
Der Eismann Kommt (O'Neill), 153
Deutsche Film-Aktiengesellschaft or DEFA, 81, 141
Deutsche Hochschule für Musik "Hans Eisler," 88
Deutsche Theaterinstitut, 73-74, 84, 101
Deutsches Nationaltheater, 97, 103
Deutsches Theater, 3, 8, 12, 14, 33, 35, 42-45, 46-48, 51-59, 62-64, 75, 79, 83, 88-91, 103, 105, 110, 113, 127, 140-142
Devrient, Eduard, 22, 28, 62,
Devrient, Ludwig, 29, 35
Diderot, Denis, 26
Die Arbeit des Schauspielers an Sich Selbst The Work of the Actor on Himself, or An Actor Prepares (Stanislavski), 71
Die neuen Leiden des jungen W (Plenzdorf), 101
Dierichs, Otto, 82
Dietrich, Marlene, 2, 58, 61
Diplom, 8, 10, 95, 108, 124, 132, 133
Doctor Faustus (Marlowe), 41
Doctor Faustus Lights the Lights (Stein/Wilson), 139
Don Carlos, (Schiller), 145
Drogi, Veronica, 133-134
Drevus, Margot, 121
Drews, Wolfgang, 57
Dumont, Louise, 62, 91

Earth Spirit (Wedekind), 42
Ekhof, Konrad, 18-20, 25, 27, 30, 33
Engelmann, Ulrich, 105, 116
Erpenbeck, Fritz, 74
Erweiterte Oberschule, 134
Espey, Lore, 84
Eugene O'Neill Theater Center, 115

Eyesoldt, Gertrud, 50-52, 83

Felsenstein, Walter, 89
Festival of Serious Fun (New York City), 139
Folkwang-Hochschule für Musik, Theater, Tanz, 13
Frankfurt Schauspielschule, 40
Freie Bühne, 33
Freie Deutsche Jugend, 141
Frisch, Efraim, 51

Gaillard, Ottofritz, 68, 71-74, 103, 110, 160
Galileo (Brecht), 98
Gast, 11
GDR, 5-7, 62-64, 70, 75, 76, 77, 79, 82, 86, 88-89, 92, 94, 104, 108, 111, 112, 116, 117, 123, 125, 146-147, 154, 157-158
Gellert, C. F., 20
Genossenschaft Deutscher Buhnenangehorigen (GDBA), 9
Georg II, Duke of Saxe-Meiningen, 2, 32, 46
German Writers Conference of 1947, 69
Geschichte der Deutschen Schauspielkunst (Devrient), 29
Gestus, 45, 134
Glaser, Margrit, 57
Goebbels, Joseph, 58
von Goethe, Johann Wolfgang, 29
Gorki, Maxim, 38
Gotthold Ephraim Lessing, 20
Gottsched, Johann, 6, 20-21, 24
Group Theatre, 2
Grundstudium, 112, 127, 137, 141, 143

Hacks, Peter, 77
Hamburg Dramaturgy, 20
Hamburg National Theatre, 23, 24, 25, 27, 34
Hamburg School of Acting, 26
Hamlet (Shakespeare), 46
Hamlet/Maschine (Shakespeare/Müller), 143, 153
Hanswurst, 19, 21
Hauptmann, Gerhardt, 38
Hauptstudium, 117, 125, 128, 137, 143
Hebbel Theater, 139
Held, Bertold, 47, 51 ,54
Hilpert, Heinz, 64
Herr Puntilla und Sein Mann Matti (Brecht), 89
Hochschule für Schauspielkunst "Ernst Busch" (HfSK), 2, 3, 4, 5, 6-11, 13, 86, 107-129, 132-137, 139-140, 144, 150-162
Hitler, Adolf, 40 51, 56-58

Hochschule der Künst, 13 137
Hochschule für Bühnenkunst "Louise Dumont, 34
Hochschule für Bühnenkunst Düsseldorf, 55
Hochschule für Film und Fernsehen "Konrad Wolf," 16, 80
Hochschule für Musik "Carl Maria Von Weber," 80
Hochschule für Musik "Felix Mendelssohn-Bartholdy," 13, 80
Hoffman, Hans-Joachim, 98
Honecker, Erich, 101
Hrosvitha, 16
Hübner, Bruno, 57
Humbolt Universität, 89, 103

Ibsen, Henrik, 38
Iffland Wilhelm, 22-25, 30
Improvisations-Seminar, 112, 136
Institut für Musik und Theater des Landes Mecklenburg-Vorpommern, 7, 16

Jessner, Leopold, 36

Kabale und Liebe (Schiller), 118
Kammerspiele, 43, 53-54, 63
Karchow, Ernst, 64
Karlsrühe Theater, 29
Kathchen of Heilbron (Schiller), 43
Kean, Edmund, 23
Kentner, Heinz Dieter, 57
Klawitter, Klaus, 134
Kleinau Willy, 83
Kleinert, Peter, 100, 111, 126-128
Kleines Theater, 47
von Kleist, Heinrich, 43
Komische Oper, 3, 128
Königliche Polizei-Prasidium, 50
Kornfield, Paul, 35
Kuhle Wampe (Brecht), 98
Kuniglich Teaterhogsköle Stockholm (State School for Theater Training, Stockholm), 88

L'Arronge, Adolf, 42
Laienspielengruppen, 136
Lang, Otto 71
Langhoff, Thomas, 94
Langhoff, Wolfgang, 62, 89 105
Laube, Heinrich, 50
Legband, Paul, 61
Leipzig Oper, 128
Leipzig School of Acting, 21

Lerner and Lowe, 122
Lessing, Gotthold, 20, 25, 26
Lienert, Frank, 143-144
Lorre, Peter, 2
Lucretia, (Sachs), 16
Lukacs, Georg, 77

Magister, 9
Mann Dieter, 140-142
Mann, Emil, 50
Mannheim Court Theatre, 23
Mannheim School of Acting, 24
Marie-Seebach Schule, 55
Marx, Karl, 63
Mathys, Thomas, 119, 136-137
Matley, Bruce, 3, 135
Maxim Gorki Theater, 3, 100, 153
Max-Reinhardt Seminar, 60
Medea, (Euripides), 42
Merchant of Venice (Shakespeare), 43
Meves, Hans-Dieter, 100
Meyenburg, Alexandra, 71
Minetti, Hans-Peter, 92-93, 108, 110
Minnich, Herbert, 119, 120-122
Miracle of the Evening, 45
Moliere, Jean Baptiste, 98
Molly Bloom,(Joyce,) 143
Morgenroth, Daniel, 27, 114, 153
Moscow Art Theatre, 2
Mother Courage and Her Children (Brecht), 75
Mühe, Ulrich, 153
Müller, Heiner 2, 116, 126, 155, 158,
Musikhochschule des Saarlandes, 16
My Life in Art *Mein Leben in der Kunst* (Stanislavski), 71

National Theaterinstitut Weimar, 88
Neuber, Caroline, 6, 20
Neue Bundesländer, 114
Neue Deutsche Literatur, 85
Neue Sachlichkeit, 77
Neues Theater, 42
Neumann, Vera, 122-123
Normalvertrag Solo, 10

Oedipus Rex, 44, 47, 56
Otte, Eva Marie, 122-125
Otto-Falckenberg-Schule, 13

Palais Wesendock, 50, 56
Palucca-Schule, 88
Peer Gynt (Ibsen), 159
Pelleas and Melisande (Maeterlinck), 47

Penka, Rudolf, 68, 83, 87-92, 100, 110-111, 161
Piens, Gerhard, 89
Piscator, Erwin, 37
Plenzdorf, Ulrich, 112, 161
positiver held, 65
Prenzlauer Berg, 99, 121, 128
Prüfungscommission, 126
Psychotechnik, 57

Radek, Karl, 67
Regelunterricht, 124
Regiebuch, 45
Regieinstitut, 111, 121
Reichersche Hochschule für dramatische Künst, 55
Reichkanzleistil, 57
Reichsministerium, 57-58
Reichsministerium für Volksaufklärung und Propaganda, 57
Reichstheaterakademie Berlin, 58
Reichstheaterkammer, 57
Reinhardt, Max, 2-4, 6, 34, 42, 45-50
von Rex, Caspar, 9, 108
Rodgers and Hammerstein, 122
Rodler, Wolfgang, 49, 116
Roos, Christopher, 139
Royal Academy of Dramatic Art, 152
Runge, Woldemar, 56

St. Denis, Michel, 99
Sachs, Hans, 18
Salome (Wilde), 42
Schall und Rauch, 41
Schaubühne am Lehniner Platz, 11
Schauspielschule der Vereinigten Stadttheater Köln, 34
Schauspielschule des Deutschen Theaters, 6, 28, , 36, 48, 57-59, 61, 75, 80, 83-84, 154-155
Schiller Theater, 68
Schlegel, Johann Elias 20
Schneider, Karl, 94
Schönemann Academy, 22
Schönemann Company, 22
Schöneweide, 90, 104, 115, 117, 121-122, 142
Schorn, Christine 142-143
Schreyvogel, Josef, 29-30
Schroeder, Friedrich Ludwig, 22
Schroeder, Sophie, 19, 26, 25
Schroth, Peter, 100
Schürmann-Horster, Willy, 58

Schubert, Götz, 153
SED, (Socialist Unity Party of Germany),69-70, 76-77, 112
Semper Oper, 129
Seyffert, Dietmar, 128-129
Shakespeare, William, 47-48, 82, 130, 136
Simmgen, Hans-Georg, 100
Socialist Realism, 65-77
Solter, Friedo, 94, 105, 110, 153-154
Sprecherziehung, 119
Skinner, Edith, 122
Staatliche Hochschule für Musik und darstellende Kunst, 13
Staatliche Musikhochschule Weimar, 71
Staatliche Schauspielschule Berlin, 3, 5-6, 61, 77, 80-81, 96, 98-99,110
Staatliche Schauspielschule Rostock, 9, 80
Staatliche Schauspielschule Wien, 54
Staatliche Theater Schwerin, 93
Staatlichen Kommission für Kunstangelegenheiten, 79
Staatsicherheit (Stasi), 101
Städtische Schauspielschule Leipzig, 35
Stalin, Josef, 72 73 75, 79
Stanislavski, Konstantin, 4, 5, 32, 39, 68, 71, 79-85, 92-96, 100-103, 111, 123, 134
Stockholm Symposium, 88, 100
Strakosch, Alexander, 50
Studiobühne "Wolfgang Heinz," 106, 109, 121
studiotheater BAT, 109-110, 118, 126
Sturm, Johannes, 19
Sturm und Drang, 28

The Last Days of the Commune (Brecht), 76
The Miracle (Reinhardt),50
The Mother (Brecht), 84
The Normal Heart (Kramer), 104
The Pelican (Strindberg),145
The Studiobühne "Wolfgang Heinz," 117
The Tempest (Shakespeare),121
The Wedding Proposal (Chekov), 89
Theater am Park, 122
Theater der Jungen Welt, 87
Theater der Zeit, 74
Theaterakademie Karlsrühe, 40, 62
Theaterhochschule "Hans Otto," 16, 87, 97, 105, 116
Theatre am Palast, 93

Über Theatreschule, 28, 54
Union of Soviet Writers 72
Universität Halle, 80
Universität Jena, 35

Universität Leipzig 89
Univerzitet Umetnosti U Beogradu (Academy for Theatre, Film, Television, and Radio Belgrad), 88
Unterwegs (Müller) 158

Vallentin, Maxim, 68, 71-73, 92, 103
Veth, Kurt, 99-100, 117, 132 155
verfremdungseffekt, 44
Versuch einer kritischen Dichtkünst für die Deutschen, 17
Virginia (Sachs), 16
Völker, Klaus, 108, 140
Volksbühne, 103, 138
Volkstheater Rostock, 138

Wahlrollenstudium, 116-117
Weigel Helene, 2
Weimar School of Acting, 26-28
Werner-Kahle, Hugo, 57, 61
Westfälische Schauspielschule, 13
Weyrach, Wolfgang, 68
Wilson, Robert, 126, 139
Winkelgrund, Rolf, 153
von Winterstein, Eduard,57, 84
Wissenschaftsrat, 9, 194

Yale School of Drama, 152

Zentrale Bühnen-Fernseh- und Filmvermittlung der Bundesanstalt für Arbeit (ZBF), 10
Zhdanov, Andrei, 66-67
Zillmer, Gertrud Elisabeth, 100

STUDIES IN THEATRE ARTS

1. J.R. Dashwood and J.E. Everson (eds.), **Writers and Performers in Italian Drama From the Time of Dante to Pirandello: Essays in Honour of G.H. McWilliam**
2. David P. Edgecombe, **Theatrical Training During the Age of Shakespeare**
3. Bryant Hamor Lee, **European Post-Baroque Neoclassical Theatre Architecture**
4. Diane Hunter (ed.), **The Makings of Dr. Charcot's Hysteria Shows: Research Through Performance**
5. Jan Clarke, **The Guénégaud Theatre in Paris (1673-1680): Volume One: Founding, Design and Production**
6. James Strider, Jr., **Techniques and Training for Staged Fighting**
7. Steve Earnest, **The State Acting Academy of East Berlin-A History of Actor Training from Max Reinhardt's** *Schauspielschule* **to The** *Hochschule für Schauspielkunst "Earnst Busch"*